D0385816

Tea Light Moments
FOR Women

Hope Lyda

HARVEST HOUSE PUBLISHERS

EUGENE, OREGON

Cover by Garborg Design Works, Savage, Minnesota

Cover photo © Garborg Design Works, Savage, Minnesota

TEA LIGHT MOMENTS FOR WOMEN
Previously published as *Tea Light Moments for a Woman's Soul* and *Tea Light Moments to Refresh Your Day.*
Copyright © 2009 by Hope Lyda
Published 2010 by Harvest House Publishers
Eugene, Oregon 97402
www.harvesthousepublishers.com

ISBN 978-0-7369-2233-3

Printed in China

10 11 12 13 14 15 16 / RDS-SK / 10 9 8 7 6 5 4 3 2 1

To Marc,
my daily reminder of God's light and grace

Contents

Light a candle and wait upon God
to strengthen your faith.
Light a candle and pray for someone else
to shift your perspective.
Light a candle and lift up your hurts
to start your healing.
Light a candle and seek forgiveness
to transform your heart.
Light a candle and listen to God
to live your purpose.

～

So now I can walk in your presence,
O God, in your life-giving light.

PSALM 56:13

God's Light

God is light.

1 JOHN 1:5 NIV

Lighting a candle beckons me to sit still. The act is peaceful and inviting. So inviting that my impulse to work, finish tasks, make a call, or roam the house deciding what to do next is extinguished. I have an external focal point that leads to the internal…the soul, the heart. And here I discover, each time, the light of God.

In the past few years a spiritual and emotional journey led me back to the practice of lighting a candle to begin a time of focused prayer. To inspire the ritual, I placed a tea light candle in front of a framed image a friend had given to me for this journey. It is a beautiful woodcut based on a Gospel story in which Jesus raises a synagogue ruler's daughter from the dead. Above the scene are the Aramaic words *talitha cumi*, which mean "maiden, rise." Beneath the black-and-white contrasted image is the title "Come forth to life." I love that. Isn't that what we all long for? Whether we need joy, hope, mercy, or strength… the steps we take in faith are steps taken toward life. Abundant life. Intentional life. Meaningful life.

My prayers were initially for healing and direction; but over time, as I struck the match and leaned in toward the wick of the tea light candle in its glass holder, many other prayers and thoughts would surface. This simple action reignited a desire to lift up my life completely to God's care.

I don't know what your journey looks like today, but I do know that the light of a single candle can help you find your way. It can lead you to times of prayer, meditation, questions, and praises. I invite you to light a candle and join me for a devotional pilgrimage through the mundane and the miraculous, the everyday and the eternal. May this gathering of observations, reflections, and prayers be a faithful companion for your life right now. I hope it inspires you to "come forth to life" in God and in meaningful ways.

Hope Lyda

Light a Candle
for Awareness

A Moment to Breathe

I make the most of all that comes
and the least of all that goes.

SARA TEASDALE

———— ❧ ————

I need just a moment. To catch my breath. To take in wonder.
To explore my thoughts. To consider my faith. To reflect on
the day. To wait and listen. When I look at my schedule and
consider how many moments come and go, wasted on mind-
less tasks or rote thoughts, it is no surprise that I feel worn out
and have very little to show for it. Moments of silence allow
us to listen for the cues and leadings that the whir of our autopilot feature tends to drown out.

What currently keeps you from silence? Is it the busyness
of your day, the rhythm of your life, the pulse of your own
expectations? Maybe the better question is: Which came first,
the avoidance of silence or the busyness? I believe our ability
to sit with the silence and in silence depends greatly on what
we experienced during our childhood. Chaos breeds chaos,
and calmness breeds calmness. However, if we experienced an
extreme of either of those, we might crave the other out of a
desire to protect or comfort ourselves. While some of us are just
more naturally inclined to crave solitude, I believe that we are
all created to experience those moments of silence and of seeking. This is when we can feel and know God's presence.

Still moments before God allow us to welcome what the day has to offer. We are less likely to cling to the burdens of yesterday or clench our fingers around today in anticipation of tomorrow's possible concerns. Honor this day. Celebrate its unfolding as you celebrate your own awakening.

Shedding Light

- Consider what keeps you from practicing moments of silence. Prepare a place or a time that allows for a bit of refuge.

- What does the clamor of your routine sound like—traffic in motion, coworkers in conference, cries of little ones, the ring of a cell phone? Wait for these sounds to settle. The voice of God is beneath them.

Prayer

God, grant me a heart, mind, and spirit that are open to all that today offers. Help me make the most of what comes my way and make the least of what goes.

Afterglow

Today I will be awake so that I can see and feel all that God reveals.

Sit with Me

Then Jesus said, "Come to me, all of you who are weary
and carry heavy burdens, and I will give you rest."

MATTHEW 11:28

Stepping into God's presence is not always easy for me. It
is never a question of his whereabouts, but of the location
of my thoughts. When I'm ready to be quiet, still before God,
my thoughts often are of me...and my list of transgressions
mostly. That ever-stinging regret turns a chance for reflection
into either a pity party or a guilt trip. So I'm either surrounded
by my liveliest, most drastic mishaps, or I'm packing up my baggage and mentally distancing myself. Neither scenario ushers
me into silence, focus, or to God's side. I *feel* that I can't enter
God's presence with these blatant flaws from my past and the
ones fresh from this morning. It *seems* a bit like joining the
queen of England for tea while wearing my favorite sweats—
the ones with holes in the knees and the hem threads draping
like fringe. It's not proper. Pious. Or very polite.

Well, here's a big difference: Chances are that the queen
isn't inviting you or me to tea. But *God is* inviting us to spend
time with him. In the blink of a spiritual background check,
he knows about those flaws and that entire year or period in
your life when you ignored him. And yet the invitation arrives

anyway. "Join me," it says. And best of all, it closes with the perfect line, "Come as you are."

Shedding Light

- What do you believe you have to achieve, do, or be before you can sit with God? Clear away those human expectations of worthiness and replace them with thoughts of God's invitation to come to him with all your burdens, flaws, and needs.

- If God calls you to him, no matter your state of imperfection, are you willing to drop everything and savor such acceptance?

Prayer

God, I come with baggage, as you know. I'll work on giving that over to you, piece by piece. Forgive me for holding back because of my feelings of unworthiness. They keep me from baring my soul. They keep me from your presence.

Afterglow

I'll stop making excuses so that I can be real before God and experience the wonder of grace.

It's Getting Crowded

If one does not know to which port one
is sailing, no wind is favourable.

SENECA

------&----------

*D*id I turn off the oven? Are my tags about to expire? Will our tree fall over with the next big wind? Let's see, if the mortgage check went through before the electrical check, I might be in trouble. Did I drink the last of the milk? I wonder how long road construction can possibly last! The price of stamps went up again…These are my thoughts in the span of a split second. Whether I'm driving to a meeting or standing in line at the grocery store or walking down the hall after a late evening trek to the bathroom, these thoughts storm through the sorely ineffective barricades in my mind and take over my conscious and subconscious life. They leave me unfocused, frazzled, and longing for direction.

It's getting too crowded in here…in my mind and heart. I'm filled and overflowing, but not with the reflections my life and spirit crave. I want to spend moments fully aware of mercy's tenderness, of God's leading, of gratitude's buoyancy. But it takes concerted effort to quiet the crowd of daily surface details and musings to get to the depths of God-thoughts. This is our chance to do just that…to make the effort toward intimacy with God. There are so many concerns and ideas worth contemplation. Wait for the crowd to die down and clear some space to explore purpose, redemption, and the joy of being alive in this moment.

If you never allow time to ponder your direction, your heart, and those deeper thoughts that rumble below the chatter of the mind, you will not be in tune with your life or the direction God is leading you.

Shedding Light

- Identify and list which reoccurring thoughts keep you up at night or interfere with your concentration during the day. Spend a few moments praying over these specific concerns.

- Was there ever a time in your life when you more readily explored questions of God, faith, and wonder? What can you do now to recapture that spiritual level of contemplation?

Prayer

Lead me to your feet, Lord. I want to sit and listen as you speak truth into my life. Keep me from crowding out those times when a song of praise rises up in my spirit or a prayer drifts from my heart to my tongue. These times will honor you.

Afterglow

I'll allow my thoughts and prayers to go deeper. I'll spend time considering more than the worldly concerns that usually occupy my mind.

The Flame of Faith

*There are two ways of spreading light: to be
the candle or the mirror that reflects it.*

EDITH WHARTON

Fire and water. These powerful elements and their attributes
often star in prose—from poetry to liturgy. They are used
metaphorically and literally to provide us with deeper understanding of our spiritual and physical lives. Many of us have
stepped forward to be immersed in water…to be baptized. To
demonstrate and complete the giving of ourselves over to God,
we rise up out of the swelling river, the splashing baptistery, or
a lake dotted with swaying boats at summer camp—and we
are a new spiritual creature, buoyed by hope and dripping in
grace. We become a part of God's light, a refraction and reflection of his shining countenance.

Because of the water, we carry the flame of faith. The ignited
torch of belief lights the way for us in times of shadows and
cascades brilliant sparks, like a Fourth of July display, when
we celebrate life's immeasurable wonder. God is our source of
light. And a life cast in reverence, joy, compassion, and belief
becomes a mirror to reflect that light within our circumstances,
our families, our circles—no matter how big or how small—
and our world.

The ebb and flow of water is much like the rise and wane of a fire. Both can carry us toward deeper belief.

Shedding Light

- What has carried you toward belief in the past and what does so today?
- Does your flame of faith burn brightly, or does it need renewal?
- Try to find ways in your everyday living to become a mirror held up to holiness.

Prayer

The elements of fire and water are nothing compared to the power of your love that illuminates this life before me. Remind me to tend to the flame of my faith so that it never subsides. May it never cast light upon my own doings but always reflect your goodness.

Afterglow

Today I light a candle. It's a simple act, but it renews my faith.

New View

Acknowledge and take to heart this day that the LORD
is God in heaven above and on the earth below.

DEUTERONOMY 4:39-40 NIV

From my perch on the penthouse level balcony of a rented urban condo, I saw a city with new perspective. It wasn't my city, but it was a city I have enjoyed numerous times by walking the steep streets for hours, observing the locals and tourists, and savoring cuisine served up at every corner. But I'd never noticed how impressively far the bay stretches beyond the celebrated shoreline market. I'd never looked up at the many birds staring down from telephone wires. And I'd never witnessed how many people crisscross intersections simultaneously seven blocks apart.

We maneuver through our days, make choices, and pursue purpose with a street-level view of living. God's eye view presents a scene much more vast and eternal. Yes, God is there with us when we walk the pavement or have our nose to the grindstone, but God also sees how failure and forgiveness intersect up ahead in our journey. He knows that the small stumbling block we dismiss today will turn into a bigger trial down the road. And when the obstacle in front of us seems insurmountable, he sees how small it is in light of his power.

He is the Lord in heaven above and on the earth below.

We live here, but our mind-set and perspective can be that of heaven, if we take time to look up now and then.

Shedding Light

- Look at life differently by depending on God's vision.
- Give whatever seems overpowering or unmanageable over to God's purpose and plan, so that he can put the situation into right perspective.

Prayer

My view is so limited. I want to trust you with every turn, every step. Guide me today and lead my human heart in the ways of heaven above. Help me understand that even when I cannot see beyond today, you see and know my future.

Afterglow

I'll look up more often...not just to take in a greater view but to call upon the One who sees all.

What Springs Up

Inside myself is a place where I live all alone, and that's where I renew my springs that never dry up.

PEARL BUCK

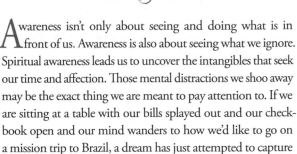

Awareness isn't only about seeing and doing what is in front of us. Awareness is also about seeing what we ignore. Spiritual awareness leads us to uncover the intangibles that seek our time and affection. Those mental distractions we shoo away may be the exact thing we are meant to pay attention to. If we are sitting at a table with our bills splayed out and our checkbook open and our mind wanders to how we'd like to go on a mission trip to Brazil, a dream has just attempted to capture our attention. Dreams, goals, life questions, and prayers emerge when we least expect them.

The multitasking nature many of us have adopted has its benefits, but what falls by the wayside are those brief encounters of understanding that surface and require more thought and consideration. We are too busy cleaning our email inbox, sending a fax, and answering our phone, so the spiritual leading gets squelched. Exchanging efficiency for spiritual deficiency is not a good trade.

Practicing awareness ultimately requires us to pay attention to these hopes and musings when they spring up. They don't come to us as whispers because they are unimportant, they emerge as whispers because they deserve our undivided, rapt, lean-on-the-edge-of-our-chairs attention.

Shedding Light

- Spend less time shooing away dreams and more time musing over them.

- When was the last time you listened to your dreams? Where did they lead?

- Can you think of an idea that you squelch on a regular basis? Give it space.

Prayer

I want to be centered and not scattered. Teach me the wisdom of silence. When my spirit resists it and I fill my time with activities and my ears with voices, music, media, and dialogue…lead me to the quiet whispers of my soul and of your will.

Afterglow

When I pay attention, I am more connected to my life and to God. I will listen for my heart to speak up today and will be prepared to take notes.

Light a Candle
for Delight

Spice It Up

Don't be afraid your life will end: be
afraid that it will never begin.

GRACE HANSEN

———— ✎ ————

Habanera, cayenne, cumin, chipotle, clove, jalapeno, cinnamon, and chile piquin. This could be the beginnings of a deadly burrito sauce, but because I'll never be someone who appears on the Food Network, this, instead, is a recipe for joy. Spice, zip, and zest might not make their way into many meditation books, but when it is time to talk about delight, we must turn to our senses. What better way to ignite them than with something that has a bit of fire? I bought a hot chocolate mix with Mexican seasonings a couple weeks ago, and it was fabulous. I instantly had a new passion (and respect) for hot chocolate, the drink formerly known as a poor substitute for good coffee.

What infuses your soul with a wonderful burst of heat and flavor? Is it a quick dive into a clear, blue pool? A splash of red on your fingernails? The idea of a Saturday road trip with no particular destination? A book, a beach, and a bottomless iced tea? The exhilaration of running along a river trail? The smile of your spouse or the tender kisses of your children? It might be something that initially scares you—like making a new friend or starting a new career. Embrace whatever adds spice to your spirit and faith. It might transform what once seemed like a poor substitute for a good life into…a good life!

Shedding Light

- Tap into whatever motivates and excites you about life—such things can be directing you to your intended passion and purpose.

- If delight seems to be something that only others experience, create your own recipe to spice up your life. Start with a challenge or a time of prayer asking for awareness.

Prayer

My bland existence is a meager offering to you, God. I want to live with vibrancy and spark. Rekindle in me the passion for living that ushers your children to a life of amazing delight.

Afterglow

I'll add seasonings and spices to my life. Out of gratitude, I'll seek to live each day with passion and wonder.

Joie de Vivre

Take delight in the LORD,
and he will give you your heart's desires.

PSALM 37:4

———— ✦ ————

Does it seem decadent to delve into the topics of desire and passion? Have a few misguided romance novels or cable channels caused us to eliminate such words from our language—even when we are talking about our spiritual journey? What an unfortunate loss! Our spiritual journeys are absolutely, undeniably, unapologetically supposed to be filled with desire and passion. And yet many of us temper our emotions, even when they swell with gratitude for all that God is and does in our lives. We walk away from hardship experienced by strangers—and sometimes even friends—because their intense need reminds us of our frailty and deep longings for acceptance and love. Instead of embracing miracles, we reduce grand, life-changing God-moments to the size of coincidence by rationalizing them with human reason or attributing them to human responsibility.

Joie de vivre, the joy of living, is not a dirty phrase, nor is it reserved for the French, though we could learn a lot from their pursuit of simple pleasures. Don't put out the fires that stir your heart and lead you to impassioned and emboldened faith. Desire leads you to find the One who can fulfill your every longing. Passion leads you to gratefully serve the One who seeks to give you the delight of your heart and soul.

Shedding Light

- What ignites your passion for living, serving, and being?
- Make the connection between your gifting and your desires. How might the gifts God has given you lead you to fulfill the desires of your heart?

Prayer

What a gift this life is! God, I want to make the most of this life you have given to me. Let my passions be yours for me. Show me how to use my gifts—to reveal and use them for godly, fulfilling purposes.

Afterglow

I will work "desire" and "passion" back into my spiritual vocabulary.

Unguarded

*When we were children, we used to think that
when we were grown-up we would no longer
be vulnerable. But to grow up is to accept
vulnerability... To be alive is to be vulnerable.*

MADELEINE L'ENGLE, *WALKING ON WATER*

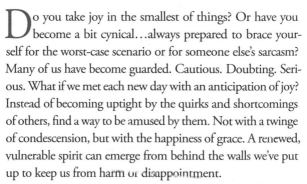

Do you take joy in the smallest of things? Or have you become a bit cynical...always prepared to brace yourself for the worst-case scenario or for someone else's sarcasm? Many of us have become guarded. Cautious. Doubting. Serious. What if we met each new day with an anticipation of joy? Instead of becoming uptight by the quirks and shortcomings of others, find a way to be amused by them. Not with a twinge of condescension, but with the happiness of grace. A renewed, vulnerable spirit can emerge from behind the walls we've put up to keep us from harm or disappointment.

When does your guard go up? With certain family members? At work? With strangers who trigger your impatience? Revisit these people or these circumstances with a refreshed spirit of joy. Let a bit of levity brighten your mood, mind-set, and manner. This becomes an act of good will and good nature that ultimately reflects God's love. Amusement will override annoyance. Wonder will outweigh worry. Self-protection will open up to compassion. And through the act of becoming vulnerable and lighthearted, you'll discover a deeper sensitivity to God's leading, wisdom, and will. You'll discover what delights await the heart that welcomes and accepts.

Shedding Light

- When do you shut yourself off or distance yourself emotionally? Try countering these situations by changing your attitude in advance.

- Lighten up whenever possible. Add more fun and laughter to your life starting this week.

Prayer

Lord, you created laughter and joy. You don't want me to wallow in complaints, insecurities, or conflict. These become my barriers to spiritual growth and delight.

Afterglow

I will release judgment of myself and others, so that I can share God's love more readily and more willingly.

Skipping and Clapping

Some pursue happiness, others create it.

AUTHOR UNKNOWN

Go to any playground, and you'll find a wisdom that surpasses any book-learning you've had. It is the understanding of unadulterated joy. Children aren't taught the ways of joy. It bubbles up from their soul and expresses itself in their broad, welcoming grins and their wide-eyed expressions of awe—both are usually followed by unaffected laughter.

What I really like to see is the way children physically throw themselves into life's delight. They don't politely smirk or chuckle. They display physical comedy like they've been training as comedians, but it's even better because it's pure in intention—they're expressing their heart's joy. They clap their hands in celebration of sunshine, flowers, bugs, or bath bubbles. They smack their lips after tasting something delicious. They hum to music—even when there is no music to be heard. They slap their hand on their short thighs like a cowboy after a good campfire joke. And they skip! They half-run, half-dance across a lawn on a Saturday afternoon or down the hallway at school to greet a friend.

Couldn't we get back to that purity somehow? Can we remember our first sips of delight? How sweet. How rich. How fulfilling. And, oh, how we wanted to share it!

Shedding Light

- Allow your joy to be shared physically—clap your hands in praise of someone's success or effort, give hugs, smile at your barista and mean it, and, if the situation presents itself, go for the skip. I'm pretty sure that even if you don't break out into pure laughter, someone will.

- Throw yourself into something that isn't about gaining success but about gaining joy and a thirst for life.

Prayer

I've tasted pure joy, but it was a long time ago. When I equate life with routine, rules, and rigidity, remind me how to play and how to be a child of God—savoring delight without shame, self-consciousness, or judgment.

Afterglow

I'll try a little physical comedy today. I'll express my joy or my affection without holding back.

Happy with the Present

*Happiness is not a state to arrive at,
but a manner of traveling.*

MARGARET LEE RUNBECK

———— ✎ ————

There is great relief to be had when we stop dictating what will give us happiness and allow God to gently, or sometimes swiftly, move us toward true contentment. There are probably as many definitions of happiness as there are people, but many of us define joy in terms of something we hope *will happen* in the future. "I would be so happy, if I got that job." "Life would be so wonderful, if I didn't have so much responsibility right now." "Once I retire the good life will begin!" "When my kids get older, I'll be able to figure out what I want my life to be."

It is fine to hope for change or for things to be different, but if these future versions of life become our only example of joy…we'll never find the happiness that God has placed all around us in our immediate circumstances. Like buried treasures they lay hidden in the people, conversations, decisions, and possibilities we encounter daily but don't recognize. "What ifs" will, over time, undermine the great "what is" of your life. If you are hard-pressed to find blessings and delight in your current circumstances, don't pray for God to fast-forward you to a new scenario—pray for God to reveal those hidden treasures as you move forward in life.

Shedding Light

- Stop waiting for happiness to come to you. Discover it in your present life.

- Consider how you've defined happiness over the years. Was that standard handed down to you by parents or by media or by career standards? Be sure you aren't borrowing someone else's version of delight, while you miss your daily opportunities to experience deep joy and satisfaction.

Prayer

God, why have I adopted such an unattainable version of happiness as my standard? I want to stop selling my life short…I want to know the depths of happiness. Help me to become a person who creates joy and who invites others to join in.

Afterglow

I will base my happiness on the security of God's love and his desire for me to know the fullness of joy.

Treasure Hunt

Don't store up treasures here on earth.

MATTHEW 6:19

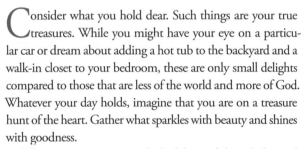

Consider what you hold dear. Such things are your true treasures. While you might have your eye on a particular car or dream about adding a hot tub to the backyard and a walk-in closet to your bedroom, these are only small delights compared to those that are less of the world and more of God. Whatever your day holds, imagine that you are on a treasure hunt of the heart. Gather what sparkles with beauty and shines with goodness.

When you encounter people, look beyond their clothes and past their initial greeting. Try to see them as a whole. What about their character is admirable and wise? Is their heart kind and generous? If you have children, think on their most wonderful traits. Before you ask your children, yet again, to do the dishes or finish their homework, be sure to tell them about the gems of delight you see in them. Invite your entire family to search for godly riches daily.

Your treasure hunt will lead you to a wealthier appreciation for life and its abundance. It will also inspire you to notice more about today and worry less about tomorrow. When you are busy gathering heavenly treasures everywhere you turn, worry cannot dominate your outlook. In fact you'll start seeing even the difficult situations in a new light.

Shedding Light

- Look for the good in others. Make it your mission to recognize strengths and abilities in anyone you meet.

- What would you hope others recognize in you as a treasure?

- Are there some earthly treasures you hold onto that get in the way of your ability to appreciate and gather godly riches?

Prayer

I want to be someone who is attracted to the good in people and in the world. I can become pretty fixated on what is falling apart or lowly gossip or the troubles that might come tomorrow. These are not worth attention or time. Remind me to pursue and acquire true treasures.

Afterglow

Today I will look for the silver linings of situations and people.

Light a Candle
for Prayer

Craving God

*Prayer is as natural as breathing,
as necessary as oxygen.*

EDITH SCHAEFFER

Have you had times when you craved communication with God? This should be our natural state of being! If and when we try to live separately from his breath, nourishment, and power, our existence is a mere shadow of the experience we are intended to have as God's creations.

Prayer is our direct connection to God's heart. Without prayer we walk through our days with a concept of God but without communion. We hold God up as deity but do not embrace him as Father. Your need for intimacy with God is as natural as your need for oxygen. Through our relationship with our Creator, we are refreshed, revived, and renewed.

Your need for the source and the source that fulfills your need do not change. Each day you require that connection all over again. Day in. Day out. When you weep privately over brokenness and pain and know that only God's presence will bring healing, you are seeking that connection. When you feel small in the world and call out for direction and meaning, you are seeking that connection. When you feel a craving deep in your spirit and an overwhelming need for God is pressed upon your heart, you have found the source for living. Breathe it in.

Shedding Light

- Do you seek connection with God only after you've exhausted everyone else on your cell phone contact list? Try him first next time.

- Brokenness and gladness alike lead us to God, if we are paying attention.

- What leads you to God? Loneliness, sadness, joy, decisions, conflict, transition? Consider these as gifts if they redirect your heart to prayer and communion with God.

Prayer

You're right there. Right here. And I still overlook the power of communion, connection, and covenant with you, God. Help me keep my focus upon you, so that my heart seeks you first in every situation.

Afterglow

I'll stop filling my need for God with everything and everyone else *but* God.

Aware of Prayer

Devote yourselves to prayer with an
alert mind and a thankful heart.

COLOSSIANS 4:2-3

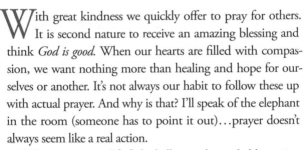

With great kindness we quickly offer to pray for others. It is second nature to receive an amazing blessing and think *God is good.* When our hearts are filled with compassion, we want nothing more than healing and hope for ourselves or another. It's not always our habit to follow these up with actual prayer. And why is that? I'll speak of the elephant in the room (someone has to point it out)...prayer doesn't always seem like a real action.

When our prayer life feels shallow, we're probably tossing out prayers halfheartedly. When our prayer life feels one-sided, we're probably not waiting to hear God's part of the conversation. God may be catching a glimpse of our heartfelt needs or our gratefulness, but we're missing out on genuine dialogue. Welcome opportunities to pray for others and your own life. Be grateful for anything that leads you to God's feet. Enter a time of prayer with an alert mind and an alert spirit...ready and waiting to receive God's compassion, love, and healing.

As you light a candle, as you carve out a still, calm moment in the day's perpetual activity, recognize your need for God in and through everything you face. Resting in the very real strength of unconditional love is the most important thing you can do today.

Shedding Light

- If prayer feels less than real, figure out what element is missing. Are you truthful when you speak to God? Are you vulnerable? Are you even talking to God or are you talking *at* God?

- Prayer doesn't require perfection, but it does require participation. Make the effort.

- Alertness doesn't come easy. Give yourself rest, nutrition, exercise, and silence and see if you are more awake for your times of prayer (and more in tune with your life).

Prayer

I will sit with you today, God, because I know that you see me, hear me, and know me. I'll sit with you because there is peace in your presence. I'll sit with you even when the right words don't come to me because I know you know my heart inside and out. I'll sit with you because it's time I recognize prayer as one of the most meaningful gifts you created.

Afterglow

I will start treating the action of prayer with more respect. I will become faithful in this way.

Simplicity of Prayer

*You can pray while you work. Work doesn't stop
prayer, and prayer doesn't stop work. It requires only
that small raising of mind to Him. "I love You,
God, I trust You, I believe in You, I need You now."
Small things like that. They are wonderful prayers.*

MOTHER TERESA

———❦———

Poignant prayers have been scribed over the ages. But such
petitions don't soar to heaven more quickly or with greater
priority than a simple prayer spoken in the middle of the day
while you drive to work, clean a bathroom, or stir-fry vegetables.
Well-crafted verses are fine to read when you want to be carried to a mood of meditation and praise, but they aren't necessary for either of those experiences to take place. How it must
delight God to hear your musings, questions, and fast words
of thanks as you go about your day. These heart-to-heart calls
strengthen the bond between Creator and creation.

What are your most frequent prayers during a day? *Thank
you. Take this from me. Help. Lead me. Forgive me. Heal me. Show
me. Carry me.* You can discover a lot about how you relate to
God by looking at how many heartfelt calls you make and of
what nature they are. You'll also see where the voids are in your
communication. If you tend to yell "help" and rarely offer up
"thanks," start to expand your gratitude during the day. If you

praise God and whistle as you work and yet rarely ask for leading, you might blissfully and blindly be traveling a path that is of your own making.

Make heart-to-heart calls a regular part of your day. Don't wait for an illuminated moment of extreme emotion or spiritual awareness. Lift up the small things as they are the foundation of our lives. They are the gifts you have to offer your God.

Shedding Light

- What are your most frequently uttered prayers? Which kind of prayers do you tend to forget about? Try to mix it up. Experience depth in your dialogue with God.

- Pray without an agenda. See what God places on your heart when you stop dictating the conversation's direction. It helps if you take time to breathe deeply and wait upon God.

Prayer

Forgive me for missing out on the wonders of prayer. I am so quick to offer up my needs that I forget to inquire about the needs of others. Or I forget to lean upon your wisdom and ask for direction as I take small and big steps forward. May I also learn to hold my tongue, so that I can feel your hold on my heart.

Afterglow

When my head takes over my time of prayer, I will stop and let my heart speak.

Lift It Up

Accept my prayer as incense offered to you,
and my upraised hands as an evening offering.

PSALM 141:2

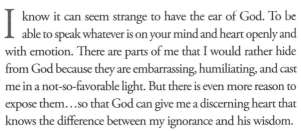

I know it can seem strange to have the ear of God. To be
able to speak whatever is on your mind and heart openly and
with emotion. There are parts of me that I would rather hide
from God because they are embarrassing, humiliating, and cast
me in a not-so-favorable light. But there is even more reason to
expose them...so that God can give me a discerning heart that
knows the difference between my ignorance and his wisdom.

Don't be afraid to be honest with the One who knows you
so very well. He has seen your flawed, regrettable moments of
acting human and self-centered, but he has also witnessed the
victorious moments when you trusted in him. Your prayers—
those authentic, difficult, and revealing prayers—are an offering
made to God. You go before him naked and dependent, and he
clothes you with compassion and mercy. Times of confession
make our times of praise that much more poignant because
we know that God's love is genuine and his grace is vast. Being
humble before the Lord is a part of prayer. Kneeling down
and bowing one's head is not an image that belongs only on
a Sunday school poster. That image should reflect the state of
our hearts as we lift up our offerings of prayer.

Shedding Light

- False humility is an obstacle to a deeper prayer life. Get real with God. What parts of your life do you hold back from sharing?

- When have you kneeled before the Lord? Try making it part of your daily prayer time. Bowing down is not merely theatrics…it is an action that leads you to a place of submission, vulnerability, and humility.

Prayer

God, sometimes I pick and choose what I bring before you in prayer. I want every aspect of my life to be under your authority and in your care, and yet I hold back. Sometimes because of fear and intimidation and sometimes because I'm lazy. I come to you today with my worries, failures, and even my shallowness fully exposed. Fill me. Teach me. I pray to be made whole.

Afterglow

I will bow down physically, spiritually, and emotionally to show my reverence for the One who hears me and loves me unconditionally.

Light a Candle
for Hope

It's Plantin' Season

*There is more hope in a fresh future. A new season
has begun, one in which I will let some fields lie
fallow while others will be prepared for planting.*

JOAN ANDERSON, *THE SECOND JOURNEY*

God will give you the seeds and the desire for the harvest
of hope to come, but you'll need to do the planting. What
is the condition of the soil of your life? Are you hardened? Are
you spiritually dry and longing for refreshment and renewal?
Have the weeds of apathy, complacency, or guilt taken root
where your hopes are meant to be firmly planted? Find ways
to tend to your garden. Have moments of meditation, spend
time in prayer, reflect on God's Word, and watch for God's
goodness to take root.

If you've experienced circumstances that have drained your
life's soil of its most vital nutrient—faith—then spend time
feeding your soul. Read inspirational writings of those who
have faced trials or droughts and who now speak of a harvest
of grace and belief. Pray your questions and ask your questions of those who know you and have wisdom. Break out of
your routine, so that the oxygen of new life breathes in and
out of your days.

Once your heart and soul are prepared to receive God's
hope for your life, you can begin sowing those precious seeds

of discipline, belief, faithfulness, and trust. Soon you will see the bright green stems rise up out of the soil and the colorful blossoms open up in full bloom. Gather them into a bouquet. And when a bloom is about to fade, there is another season of growth awaiting you in the garden. Gather another bouquet just as remarkable as the first. This is the bounty of hope. Keep planting and wait upon God for the harvest of hope fulfilled.

Shedding Light

- If there is anything keeping you from cultivating hope, try to weed it out of your life. Clear a space to plant the seeds God gives to you.

- Hope is not in limited supply. If the hope of your youth has faded, seek the new colorful harvest God intends for you to have during this time.

Prayer

I don't necessarily feel despair, and yet my life seems low on hope. Even though I send up prayers with faith, I don't always plant the discipline, belief, faithfulness, and trust that you give to me. Help me be a more diligent gardener, so that the harvest of my life reflects your bounty.

Afterglow

I won't treat hope like a rare flower anymore. I'll pluck it up every chance I get and return for more.

Innocence

*There is a divine plan of good at work in my life.
I will let go and let it unfold.*

RUTH P. FREEDMAN

When the world encounters innocence, it wants to call it naïve and out of touch. The world wants to tear it down by listing evidence of disappointment and pain. Innocence looks cheery, red-cheeked, optimistic, and shiny. Our tendency is to be skeptical of such a pure presentation.

Maybe at one time you were that fresh face of innocence. Was your heart so full of hope and possibility that you couldn't wait to spread the news of such wonder? Did doubt or hardship cause you to hold back your hope just a little and then a lot? It can happen to even the most faithful believers. In fact it can more easily happen to the most faithful believers because they are the ones who are putting themselves out there with a fragile heart full of hope.

Life isn't always fair or right or righteous, but this doesn't mean that we should dismiss innocence as a sweet but misguided quality. Innocence sees the good in circumstances and doesn't give up searching for that act of kindness or that ounce of compassion in a stranger's face. Innocence might get smudged along the way, but its shiny hopefulness is never diminished because its light burns from within and is fueled by the God of hope, the God of peace, and the God of grace.

Shedding Light

- Are you the one who has an innocent, pure sense of life, or are you the one who convinces others that they need to toughen up or "get real"?

- Give your wounds to God. Allow innocence back into your life.

Prayer

God, help me to spot innocence and try to preserve it. Don't let me give up on people or on the chance to encounter goodness and wholeness. My heart has been broken, but you have moved me beyond that point of hurt. Give me the courage to return to full living by hoping for the best and seeing the best in others and in the fresh face of each new day.

Afterglow

I will be less of a naysayer and will say more in support of innocence, purity, grace, and kindness.

Hope for the Modern World

In spite of everything I still believe that people are really good at heart. I simply can't build up my hopes on a foundation consisting of confusion, misery and death.

ANNE FRANK

As I walk by a contemporary sculpture on my way down a city street, the afternoon sun causes the creation to shimmer. It is of three whimsical figures pieced together with metal of various shapes. Each figure has its own special characteristics, but they all have something in common—their "arms" are spread wide open. When I look back at the structure from a lower point along the hill, it reminds me of Calvary, and I find myself drawn to its simple power. Regardless of the artist's intention, I am moved by the idea of a modern Calvary.

I think of how intertwined my life is with Christ's suffering on Calvary and how this advent in the Christian faith is ultimately one of hope and resurrection, not death and destruction. We are creatures pieced together by the Artisan's hand. We are called to be shining crosses that radiate with wonder and who, with arms outstretched to friends and strangers alike, become three dimensional reminders of the Calvary message our modern culture so desperately needs. Some people might walk on by. Some may never take notice. Others might dismiss you as a strange interpretation. But others will be drawn to the simple power, and their lives will forever be changed by eternal hope.

Shedding Light

- Have you made faith so complex that you have missed the simple power and beauty of the cross?

- Do you take time to see yourself as the Artist sees you?

- How can your life reflect hope and resurrection? What would that look like?

Prayer

Creator, your hands formed me, and you placed me here in this time and place and circumstance. Open up my heart to care deeply for everyone who comes into my life, whether for the long term or for a fleeting moment.

Afterglow

I will open my arms and heart wide to bring the message of Calvary to others.

Intentional Waiting

If we could for a moment see the cosmic implications
of our waiting with and for God, we would be
astonished at the glory of "ordinary" things in
our lives, and the significance of other people.

ISABEL ANDERS, *AWAITING THE CHILD*

I f we were in control, we would collect all those minutes "lost" while stopped at traffic lights, on hold on the phone, and waiting in lines and deposit them back into our life account. But thankfully that isn't an option. If we pay attention, these occasions of worldly waiting are a training ground for spiritual waiting. Maybe there is no differentiating between the two. All forms of waiting become a spiritual practice because they require us to recognize that we are not in control—one of the hardest lessons we'll ever face.

But when we wait with and for God, there are even more important lessons to embrace. We discover that there is beauty in our wounds. We learn to accept gracious help from others rather than pride ourselves in our independence. During our wait for physical healing, we learn more about our need for spiritual healing. As we long for transformation, God grants us a vision of hope to carry us and those around us. When waiting feels less than divine, we have the opportunity to see how complete reliance on God is an extraordinary gift. And when we long for God's leading but end up waiting and wondering if it is all in vain, the One who is in control makes a deposit of faith in our life accounts.

Shedding Light

- See waiting as an opportunity to grow spiritually.

- How has independence kept you from full reliance on God?

- What are you waiting upon God for right now? Pray specifically for this during your waiting moments throughout the week.

Prayer

I have allowed my distorted sense of priority to dictate how I view waiting. I get frustrated when I am asked to slow down or to hold back from rushing forth with my plan and agenda. God, pace me. Show me the rhythm of life that leads to greater understanding of you. Teach me the spiritual blessing of waiting.

Afterglow

I'll spend time deliberately looking for the glory in the ordinary.

Hope Recycled

May all who fear you find in me a cause for joy,
for I have put my hope in your word.

PSALM 119:74

How do you get hope? Do you receive encouragement from the comments of others, the support of family, the network of friends you have created? When you face trials, are you drawing on the strength and sustenance from God's Word? Are there ways you commune with God that offer renewal and restoration?

You are fortunate to have faith and hope. Many people have not yet discovered their way to renewal and the promise of grace. The great thing about hope is that it is a reusable and renewable resource. Quite a rarity for something that is such a hot commodity. But if you don't draw from your reserves and offer it to others, you are halting the cycle that God intended for the things of hope. Consider how many people you encounter each day who are eager for any remnant of peace they can hold in their hearts. What good does it do anyone if you provide an example of a life lived in hope and yet you do not share the source?

Think of how you first found hope. Who passed it on and took time to share it? Who was willing to recycle the gift of security, possibility, and faithfulness when you needed it most?

Watch for opportunities to do the same for anyone God brings into your life. Reduce your inhibitions and open up about your faith. Reuse the encouragement you've experienced. And recycle the hope of God's limitless love.

Shedding Light

- When have you withheld hope? When have you passed it along?

- Is it an inner-conflict, a deeply rooted fear, or a strong stubbornness that keeps you from freely sharing hope, hopefulness, and the peace of faith? Ask yourself why you do hold back.

Prayer

You've seen me do it before. I've started to reach out, and then in an instant, I pull back the offering of hope I was about to make. Sometimes my insecurities about faith prevent me from sharing who you are. I want to rest in your love and ignore the fears and doubts that challenge my desire to connect. Better yet I want to replace those fears and doubts with peace and never hesitate to share the endless gift of hope.

Afterglow

I'll question why I hold back from reaching out today. I won't let that become my nature.

The Science of Hope

*Hope begins in the dark, the stubborn hope
that if you just show up and try to do the
right thing, the dawn will come. You wait
and watch and work: you don't give up.*

ANNE LAMOTT

In junior high science class, a friend and I decided to do our own experiment in addition to the assigned one. We were working with seeds and petri dishes. The specifics escape memory. But what I do recall was entering the science room each day and heading straight to the formerly unused drawer, discreetly opening it up, and checking on our sprouting seedling. I think it struck us as funny to have this private experiment actually growing and probably doing better than the one we would be graded on, but there was also the thrill of creating something out of nothing. Or so we thought. We, of course, started with a seed—a seed that was already designed to grow. We were not practicing deep science as much as we were recording the journey of hope.

It turns out that our hope in Christ is a lot like that experiment. There are times when we are in the dark. We experience bouts of grief, disconnection, depression, sorrow, loss, or doubt, and the light we once walked in seems to fade with each passing day. Maybe you are going through such a season right now. Take heart. When we carry God's hope, it is with us in the dark. It is never dormant. It waits beside us and slowly grows, day by day, even in the absence of visible light. There is nothing that can separate us from the science of hope—it is already designed to grow within us.

Shedding Light

- Has darkness covered you this year? What evidence of hope has taken root in that darkness?
- You might be called upon to help a friend or even a stranger wait in the darkness. Are you prepared to sit with them and be part of the hope that is rising in their life?

Prayer

I'm designed to grow in your love and strength. God, have mercy on me in these times of darkness. I fumble along, striving to see shapes that are familiar and signs of what might lie ahead. I forget to look within…at the seeds already planted in me. You work such wonders in my life. When I feel like quitting, help me remember that I'm designed to be one of your miracles.

Afterglow

When night covers my life, I'll put fear aside and watch for the dawn.

Light a Candle
for Compassion

Upon a Star

I believe in prayer. It's the best way we
have to draw strength from heaven.

JOSEPHINE BAKER

———⟡———

Stars guided shepherds in the time of Christ. Stars still orient sailors and hikers and help fishermen make their way through the night. Their usefulness is commendable. But it is their other role that makes me a fan. When they wink and glitter against the dark sky, they invite us to speak our hearts. Did you ever close your eyes and wish upon a star for a pink-frosted birthday cake or a chance to meet your favorite singer? The expression of even small hopes is a tender act of faith.

Prayers of adulthood are more wonderful than wishes of childhood because we know who hears these pleas, requests, and expressions of happiness. And we know that our wishes don't rise a mere 500 feet in the air and dissipate into the atmosphere. They soar with clarity all the way to the ear of God, and he gladly hears them—silly, serious, deep, or simple.

In the middle of a very hard year, I lifted up prayers for simple things like open parking places, sunshine, and afternoons of solitude. God knew that I had more important things to pray about because he was the One covering me through the difficulties. But as these lighter wishes left my lips, I doubt he was concerned about my shift toward shallow. I believe he had compassion for the woman with her eyes closed and her heart open who was asking for help to make her way through the day.

Shedding Light

- Keep your connection with your Creator throughout the day by allowing your heart to speak freely and frequently.

- What is your adult equivalent of a pink-frosted birthday cake? Make a wish, say a prayer.

- Receive God's compassion in your life. Your small and big concerns matter deeply to him. He awaits those late-night, whispered prayers.

Prayer

My prayers as a young girl were true and pure. I've lost that a bit along the way. I've probably tried to impress you with my theology. Such a loss it is to stop speaking of my heart's big and small desires and hopes. God, I want to be that young girl again in spirit. I want to look to you with big eyes and an open heart and share about my day.

Afterglow

I'll allow the childlike, simple wishes to lead me to deeper faith.

Humble Pie

*Always be humble and gentle. Be patient with each other,
making allowance for each other's faults because of your love.*

EPHESIANS 4:2

Apple pie is extra tasty with a dollop of ice cream. But humble pie is made to be served with a side of compassion. Why do humility and compassion go together so well? Have you ever eaten "humble pie"? Have you ever had to go to another person or to a group and admit to a mistake, a sin, a failing, and accept the consequences? It is an uneasy, painful, and revealing process.

Your heart is never the same after being humble before others. Some people become hardened and angry because wounds are exposed when pride is stripped away; these are the people who mistakenly ordered their humble pie with a side of revenge. They think the act of humility destroys their dignity when, in fact, humility served with compassion restores dignity after ego, judgment, or greed undermines it. The heart becomes softer when one's eyes are opened up to the purpose for compassion. Human compassion welcomes others into its embrace even as we struggle to accept ourselves as fallible. God's compassion covers us when we deserve to wallow in our man-made pit of despair.

God will accept your meager words and your broken

thinking and mend you from the inside out. There is no room for spite when a heart is filled with grace and understanding. Those who have tasted compassion, when they deserved nothing but punishment or ridicule, become the people who forever serve the Lord with passion and who bestow compassion on others readily.

Shedding Light

- Seek God's help to shed pride, so that you can know the humility of a servant's heart.

- When are you most full of pride and boasting? Is it when you are at work, with family, among friends, or when you are among strangers and feeling insecure?

- Approach your pride-triggered situations with a heart of compassion. Put God's love in the space between you and other people, so that there is no room for your insecurities.

Prayer

I humble myself before you, God. I am proud and stubborn and independent. I've even ignored the needs of others because I've been focused either on my abilities or my inabilities so much that I don't recognize the opportunities for compassion and grace. Show me how to extend grace to others and to myself.

Afterglow

I will stop protecting myself from the responsibility of asking for forgiveness or acting with humility, so that I can know grace.

Dog Shopping

Change really becomes a necessity
when we try not to do it.

ANNE WILSON SCHAEF

For years I've ignored my husband's comments about how our yard is *perfect* for a dog. And when he gets the cats to act like canines by training them to do tricks before they are allowed out the back door, I just smile and pretend that's normal.

I prefer to cohabitate with cats. We have one sweet one and one neurotic one, and that suits me fine. We can pile food in the dish, refresh the water, tidy the box, and say "See you when we get back, girls" as we head out for a weekend. A dog would be a lot of work and would require so much more attention and planning.

There are many logical reasons not to get a dog, but I want to let go of self-protection philosophies and tactics that keep me from embracing change. I want to believe that good things come not only when I simplify life but when I am willing to expand it. I want to be compassionate enough to make choices that include the visions and hopes of others. For example, the cats will appreciate being cats rather than stand-ins for dogs. And my husband will have the joy of a wish fulfilled.

When we finally find "the one" and the volunteer at the

shelter looks at me and my sweater laced with cat hair, I plan to go the way of hope and kindness and boldly say:

"I want a dog. Please."

Shedding Light

- What don't you want to do? Is it because you fear change? Is it because you don't want to give in? Release your hold and see what might unfold.

- Sometimes standing firm in our ways and in our opinions and beliefs is just an overly righteous way to remain frozen, unable to grow or trust.

Prayer

Okay, so I'm holding onto something for the wrong reasons. You've seen me this way before…when I've said no to your calling because I was too intent to follow my preferred path or place in life. I don't want to miss out on the adventure of trusting you with what comes next. Let my life open up to the unknown.

Afterglow

I'll risk failure or mistakes if it means I have a chance at the abundant life of faith.

Pre-Ramble

*A loving silence often has far more power to heal
and to connect than the most well-intentioned words.*

RACHEL NAOMI REMEN

———— ❧ ————

Words get in the way of communicating compassion. We get in the way of communicating God's heart for others. Have you ever tried to express your sorrow, only to have a friend interrupt and introduce her struggle and sadness? I've done it to others, and I've had it done to me. I think it is a natural response. It probably comes from a desire to connect with the other person's need. That's the forgiving viewpoint. After all, what says "I understand" better than explaining our own encounter with a similar problem, plight, or loss? And doesn't it say we understand *more* than others if we also talk about our cousin's journey through the same thing, how we were by her side, even when it cost us time and energy that we'll never get back?

Nope.

Compassion doesn't have to be communicated along with your bio, resume, family tree, or pain credentials. Others don't always need hard proof that you can empathize. They need gentle proof, the kind that comes with nods, hugs, and prayers. There are times when your testimony will give great relief and comfort to another person. But before you begin to speak, take time to listen. Listen to a wounded friend's words and body

---

language. Don't rush the person toward a resolution for their situation because there might not be one…not today. And don't force your own tidy answers onto another's difficult circumstance, or you'll stifle their willingness to share their doubts and deepest needs.

Most importantly, when they struggle to find the right words, stand with them in silence. When it feels uncomfortable, that is the beginning of true empathy. Often it is in the silence that a heart awakens to God's healing.

Shedding Light

- How uncomfortable are you with the silence of another? Is it your pain or your friend's pain that you rush to cover with words?

- Consider several ways to show compassion to another that do not involve words, but only actions, thoughts, or prayers.

Prayer

When I am the person in need of the healing silence of compassion and friendship, I first seek you and your presence. You offer a balm that eases my deepest worry, my sharpest pain. I look for this care from others and sometimes it is there, sometimes it cannot be found. Give me a discerning heart when I am around anyone who weeps or who longs to weep.

Afterglow

I'll learn the languages of sorrow and of comfort and become proficient at listening to both.

Mighty Mercy

*To love deeply in one direction makes
us more loving in all others.*

ANNE-SOPHIE SWETCHINE

I watched the tide come in with awe. A bazillion drops of water form a wall that swells, climbs, rolls, and then pushes in one direction toward the shore. It is futile to try and stand against one of these big waves; it will carry you in its intended destination.

Farther down the beach, there are high sand plateaus and lower pits, the water does not come as a unified wall. It pools and swirls. There are small waves within larger waves and they grab at random sections of the shore. There is force, a powerful undertow churns, but there is no unity.

God's mercy is a mighty wave in our lives. And when we love in that one direction, in the direction God's mercy and love is flowing, we too become part of that powerful wave. If our love is scattered, random, and only doled out to a select few, our love becomes a conflicted, unpredictable force like the undertow. I challenge you to love God wholly and completely. Give yourself over to his mighty mercy. It is powerful enough to carry you to its intended destination—love.

Shedding Light

- What do you love so strongly that you get caught up in the power and direction of that love?

- Have you been caught in the undertow, unable to choose a direction or reach the shore of a goal or a dream?

- Have you let love wash over you? Allow yourself to feel God's love that fully today.

Prayer

When I try to stand against the wave of mercy, it isn't long before I feel the power of your love working through the situation. I am called to fall back into your strength and follow the way to love. Thank you for carrying me. For leading me with strength and compassion, so that I can experience your grace, not only personally, but as it extends to those around me.

Afterglow

I will give myself over to loving deeply, no matter the risk, no matter the fear, no matter the doubt…I will follow the way of God's mercy.

Birds of a Feather

*Two people are better off than one, for they
can help each other succeed. If one person
falls, the other can reach out and help.*

ECCLESIASTES 4:9-10

As the change of season brought sunnier weather, my
friend enjoyed the opportunity to sit outside and be
entertained by the sweet birds that emerged simultaneously
with the colorful new blossoms that bordered the yard. The
feathered, lively tourists congregated daily around her pond
and drank, ate, and bathed with contentment. After several
days my friend noticed that these birds had a built-in system
of support and protection. One bird always stood "guard"
while its peers took care of life's necessities.

In our lives we face many changes of season. Whether the
change is brought on by age, loss, transition, or opportunity,
we rely on the flock to help us along. Maybe someone drives
you to the doctor's office, a neighbor watches the kids on short
notice, or a friend delivers dinner when life is just plain overwhelming. The family we are born into as well as the one we
create present a way for us to experience God's support and
protection. We all need friends who stand with us or for us
and who have our back while we take care of life's necessities.

And we all need to be that friend when one of our own faces their challenge of change—big or small.

Shedding Light

- What season are you facing? What seasons are your friends and family members facing?

- Do you entrust your times of hardship or change to your "flock"?

- Do you entrust your seasons to God?

Prayer

Give me the strength I need to make it through this transition. I have hope for tomorrow even as I struggle with today. You have blessed me with friends and family who seek the best for me. I pray that I am willing to share my burdens with this support network…and may I come to you with my every need.

Afterglow

I'll accept help today. And I will humbly accept the prayers and support of those you bring into my life.

*Light a Candle
for Creativity*

Dawdle

*So you see, imagination needs moodling—long,
inefficient, happy idling, dawdling and puttering.*

BRENDA UELAND

———— ✺ ————

I used to be an expert dawdler. As a kid I loved to get lost
in music and books—they transported and filled me. I'm
sure there are arguments against cultivating a mind that so readily goes to the interior, but it was the beginning of my quest
for creativity and invention.

Sadly the world of adulthood has shifted me toward produc-
tivity, deadlines, tasks, and a preference for getting things done.
This way of life doesn't nourish my soul. I've lost the ability to
quickly and gladly settle into a vacation day or a book. Worries
override my ability to imagine my day differently. I want to see
my life with fresh eyes and a creative mind each morning.

Learn to dawdle with me. Whether you were ever good at
it or not, we should give it a try. Sitting in silence can work.
Lighting a candle is a start. Gazing at the moon for 15 minutes
after the rest of the household is asleep is fabulous. Heading
to your backyard with a glass of lemonade and a book is right
on track. Lying in a hammock while your mind drifts to how
you'd like to grow your garden next year is perfect. When you
catch yourself trying to rush by a slower person at the grocery
store or along the river path, hold back. Breathe in. Walk to

match their pace. They might be an expert dawdler, and you could learn a lot.

Shedding Light

- Have you been able to dawdle as an adult? Were you able to as a child?

- What frees you? Is it a palate of vibrant colors? An afternoon of no responsibility? A warm, lazy summer's day? A blank page in a sketch book? Discover what sparks your sense of creativity and frees your spirit.

- What keeps you from savoring life? Spend time exploring the obstacles, so that you can overcome them and fill your life with more whimsy and wonder.

Prayer

God, help me to still my spirit. Guide me toward the deeper waters of stillness and reflection. Show me how to make the most of an afternoon by "wasting" it with nothing planned. May I use the gift of dawdling to praise you, serve you, and discover more about life's riches.

Afterglow

Even if I have to schedule it…I will take time for dreaming, napping, staring at flowers, drawing scribbles, skipping stones, or whatever strikes my fancy.

Watching for Your Cue

No matter what happens, keep on beginning and failing. Each time you fail, start all over again, and you will grow stronger until you find that you have accomplished a purpose––not the one you began with perhaps, but one you will be glad to remember.

ANNE SULLIVAN

The curtain opens and reveals a stage full of musicians sitting with backs straight and bows and hands poised above instruments. The musicians don't scan the audience, they intently watch the conductor and await their cue to begin the music. And when it begins, it fills the concert hall with the sounds of grace and light.

When we struggle to live an inspired, creative life, it might be because we are looking to the crowd for approval or permission. Instead of allowing ourselves to do what we love, we take a survey of our closest friends (and critics) or of the pop culture to see if our pursuits have merit.

I can tell you—without taking the survey—that those longings have great worth and validity. Go ahead and draw, even if your last picture was of a neon green cow and a purple, oblong moon. Feel free to write, especially if your eighth-grade English teacher said you lacked imagination. If you were known as the neighborhood klutz, take a few spins about the living room.

Decorate your bedroom in a color that nurtures you even if it is off-trend. This is living a life of explored beauty.

And when you get stuck in judgment, sit at attention and keep your eyes on the Conductor to await your cue. He'll direct you to create something of grace and light that could only come from your inspired soul.

Shedding Light

- When have you sought permission before exploring an area of interest or passion? How did that turn out?

- Which activities connect you to a sense of God's delight? Create the opportunity for these activities and make them a greater part of your life.

- Become familiar with beauty by seeking it in others and in yourself.

Prayer

God, help me embrace joy. I let today's worries overcome me. I let the questions about tomorrow override my happiness. Lead me to the creative part of me that I've stifled with to-do lists, expectations, and regulations. Help me find the passions you have planted in the deepest part of my soul.

Afterglow

I'll take my cues from God. I won't take my cues from critics and complainers.

Language of the Soul

Dance is the hidden language of the soul.

MARTHA GRAHAM

———◦———

Today's a day to get out and move. Become aware of your body and how it connects you to your mind, heart, hopes, and to God. That sounds like an overstatement of benefits, but it isn't. If we consider movement only physical in nature then we miss out on much joy and wisdom—the very aspects that could inspire you to move more often. Martha Graham said that dance is the language of the soul. She wasn't a theologian, she was a dancer. And she experienced the heart's ability to express itself when a person uses rhythm instead of reason and leaps instead of logic.

Moving loosens up the body and then dislodges those stubborn bits of anger, worry, frustration, or grief that can build when we leave them to sit like stones in the stomach. Many women use their time of walking as a time to pray. It's a perfect combination. While our limbs, muscles, and bones join together to send us in a particular direction, our spirits can seek direction from God.

As an observer and introvert, I like to sit and reflect. But when I force myself out for a walk, I find that the creative juices start flowing. Ideas, connections, theories, prayers, and answers bubble up to the surface. It's as if the mind and spirit join in as soon as the feet start moving. Step on out there and see what comes to mind and spirit when you show God gratitude for your intricate, miraculous body by using it.

Shedding Light

- Find a way to move and a time to move that allows you to spend time processing, creating, and praying.

- Avoid the inclination to mask your thoughts with music or television while you are moving. Take the creative jaunt outside and stay tuned in to what comes up from within and what you experience during your encounter with your chosen environment.

Prayer

Speak to me, God. I want to feel your voice inside of me. I want to stop rushing around and start moving intentionally. Give strength to my body and soul as I make adjustments in my life. I want more creativity in my life. I want to be open to your leading. May my thoughts turn to you as soon as I step outside and walk forward with hope and without an agenda.

Afterglow

Today I will breathe in and out while moving my body and loosening up the inner areas of my heart, mind, and soul.

Powered by Optimism

No pessimist ever discovered the secret of the
stars or sailed an uncharted land, or opened
a new doorway for the human spirit.

HELEN KELLER

If God says "go," do you take a step back, so that you can weigh the pros and cons? And do you come up with a whole lot more cons each round? Even people who have the strength of hope and faith find themselves restricted by their limited attitudes. Along the way many of us learn to fear new things and avoid uncharted territory.

Pessimism causes us to see a very narrow slice of what life is and can be. Chances are that God is directing you beyond that narrow slice...and beyond your comfort zone. What good is it to say that you are someone who relies on the love and guidance of God in one breath and then say "no" to every opportunity to actually rely on the love and guidance of God?

When life is going well, we don't want to rock the boat. And when life is a bit rocky, that's when we say, "See, life is hard and unpredictable. I should stick with what is safe right now." This is not a life lived in God's power. This is a life fueled by fear. Commit today to living a life powered by optimism and hope. Reject the voices of the past or even the resumé that shows you

---

have stumbled. After all, those have no power anymore. In you God has created a new life. Live it.

Shedding Light

- When have you made choices fueled by fear? Fueled by faith? How are these experiences different?

- List your biggest fears. Face them so that they do not sneak up on you. Don't dwell on them but pray for the spiritual antidote to that fear. For example if your fear is that you will never be loved, pray to feel the presence of God's love in new ways. If you fear that something bad might happen to you, pray for protection but also pray for a deeper reliance on God—the kind that will carry you when circumstances are difficult.

Prayer

My fears blur together. I hardly know what I am specifically afraid of anymore. I feel uneasy and often worry. God, pull me out of this way of thinking and living. I want to rest in your peace and your will. Confidence gained through faith will lead me to a much more authentic life than one controlled by concern. I trust you. I lean on you.

Afterglow

I'll step out of my comfort zone today to see how big life is beyond my limited scope.

Courageous Creativity

*Each of us has an inner dream that we can unfold
if we will just have the courage to admit what
it is. And the faith to trust our own admission.
The admitting is often very difficult.*

JULIA CAMERON

———— ⌾ ————

Is there a dream that God has given to you that makes you
smile when you think of it? What keeps you on this side of
fulfilling it? It becomes easy to stifle a dream by holding it too
close. Share it and it has the space to grow. If the dream doesn't
seem complete in your mind's eye, you're probably right. Most
great ideas present the initial impetus for something bigger. The
missing pieces will come into view once you put that dream out
into the world. You might have half of an idea and someone you
meet in three months might have the other half. Or something
you are going to learn in the near future might give your dream
more dimension and direction. The lesson God gives you today
might be in preparation for the fulfillment of this dream.

Do you have gifts and talents that you'd like to use more
often? Do you feel the tug to step into a leadership role with
a ministry or an organization that touches your heart? Have
you walked by a house in your neighborhood numerous times
and wished that you had the guts to introduce yourself to the
woman who lives there? Your dream might be as simple as

finding a friend or as involved as starting a business. Small or big…dreams begin with the courage to recognize what God is building in your heart. They unfold when we confess them as a possibility!

Shedding Light

- Make a mental list of your hopes. Choose one or two and then reveal your "secret" to a mentor, a group of girlfriends, or to your spouse.

- See how the people you encounter and the things you learn today could relate to the dream that God has placed on your heart. Be attentive to the unfolding!

Prayer

Help me see how you are working in my life and the lives of others. I will give you praise for this journey I am on because I am dependent upon you and your strength. I won't ever know what tomorrow holds, but I will know that you are here with me, you see the big picture, and you have known of me and my life before I even existed. I can't wait to see how the dreams you give to me become experiences that lead me closer to your heart.

Afterglow

Today I will watch as you shape my dreams and bring new ones before me.

Start a Trend of Truth

*When a woman tells the truth, she is creating
the possibility for more truth around her.*

ADRIENNE RICH

You are a creator. You are an artist forming her life's work under the instruction of the Master. What you put out into the world is your creation. When you work hard to establish a comfortable, caring atmosphere in your home, you are creating a sanctuary. If you raise children to love others and to celebrate God, you are inspiring faith. When you speak kindness and peace into the lives of people who face pain and turmoil, you're inventing a life of compassion.

What you do today can set the trend for those around you. I love the fruit of the Spirit from Galatians 5:22-23. Let's look at them afresh as the materials God gives you, so that you can create a life's work that is honorable and holy. Love allows you to honor all of God's children. Joy celebrates life, and peace leads you back to God's presence. Patience waits for God's leading. Kindness reaches out without discrimination. Goodness inspires greatness in others, and faithfulness does not waver in the face of fear or insecurity. Gentleness eases the soul, and self-control reflects discipline and commitment.

Create a life that draws out your best and stirs a heart of faith in others. Create a breathtaking portrait of the Master.

Shedding Light

- What are you creating? What have you created?

- Return your thoughts to the fruit of the Spirit daily. Find ways to express each of them through your actions, your intentions, and your efforts.

- Let go of behaviors that do not reflect the fruit of the Spirit. Pray them away. Pare them away.

Prayer

I'm such an inconsistent role model. Help me become whole, balanced, consistent, and true in all that I do and say and profess. Where I am weak, help me glean strength through my trials and questions. Where I am false, help me dig deeper until I uncover the root of my insecurity and exchange it for your truth.

Afterglow

I will find ways to create goodness. I will find ways to inspire truth.

Light a Candle
for Purpose

The Way of Light

*Simplicity is an ongoing process, a joyful experience of
detaching ourselves from what is less important and
attaching ourselves to that which is more important.*

BARBARA DeGROTE-SORENSEN, *'TIS A GIFT TO BE SIMPLE*

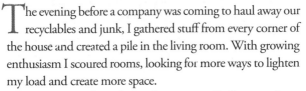

The evening before a company was coming to haul away our
recyclables and junk, I gathered stuff from every corner of
the house and created a pile in the living room. With growing
enthusiasm I scoured rooms, looking for more ways to lighten
my load and create more space.

It's surprising how things that are initially functional can
become a burden. That candy dish you bought at Cape Cod
was a prize find—now it's hidden in a cupboard behind your
broken alma mater coffee mug and a hen-shaped egg timer, and
it's in the way of pans you *do use*. It's time for it to go.

A similar fate awaits many intangibles we acquire—habits,
routines, or ruts. Behaviors that once were functional may now
be a burden. Even dysfunction serves a function initially. We
gather attitudes, defense mechanisms, or lies that help us feel
safe or in control. But when we give control over to God, the
purging needs to take place, and it needs to continue. Every day
we can eagerly and gratefully round up our sins, imperfections,
and broken pieces and toss them onto a pile. And every day
God is there to haul away our useless stuff, replacing it with

peace, light, a pure heart, and plenty of room for future good stuff. All it takes is a willingness to simplify this life you lead, so that you have room for the life God calls you to lead.

Shedding Light

- How do you burden your life with stuff? With busyness? With noise? What choices can you make to lighten your life today?

- Which habits from a life before faith still crowd your life today? How can you let go of them?

- Do you hold onto your sins and failings as tightly as you hold onto stuff? Release emotional burdens to God today.

Prayer

My life has become cluttered and chaotic because I don't let go of those things that serve no purpose. Help me to recognize those actions or beliefs that actually prevent me from purpose. I want to give these over to you. I want to stop depending on temporal pleasures or pursuits and make space for a life of eternal importance.

Afterglow

I will purge three things this week, and I will pray to release three unhealthy behaviors as well.

Anywhere But Here

*There is no need to go to India or anywhere else to find
peace. You will find that deep place of silence right
in your room, your garden or even your bathtub.*

ELISABETH KÜBLER-ROSS

This can't possibly be where God wants me! Do you ever think
this? Do you look around and wonder how you ended up
"here"—a place in life and time that falls short of your dreams
or goals? Or maybe you've achieved your aspirations, and they
have not offered the fulfillment they promised when they were
far off in the distance, dangling like a carrot.

We can find disappointment anywhere…including where
we aren't. I wish that settling into our purpose was merely a
matter of gathering up our belongings, sending out change of
address cards, and carting furniture, a few books, and a favorite lamp to another location. But that would be trying to force
a physical answer to address the spiritual question: How can
I find contentment and meaning in my current life and circumstance?

First we need to stop looking "elsewhere" because that leads
us to deceive ourselves into believing that happiness can *only*
materialize somewhere else. It also causes us to stop believing in God's amazing power to change our lives and perspec-
tives. Next we need to look to where there is contentment and

meaning—in God's peace and will. And last of all, take your discouragement or apathy—or whatever it is that first caused you to doubt—to God and watch him turn it into something useful for your journey of purpose: hope, understanding, discernment, grace, peace, anticipation, or wonder.

Shedding Light

- Seek refuge in your own life for awhile. Give yourself the gift of time and nurturing.

- Light a candle, say a prayer, and step into rituals that breathe life back into your day and renew your sensitivity to God's gentle leading.

- What version of life do you pine for? Start investing in what is going on here and now. Things can and will change, but not if you stop working on your life as it is.

Prayer

When my hopes became a long list of wants that left me feeling dissatisfied, they stopped being a part of my faith. They became excuses for me to complain. You have shown me that dreams can inspire my daily living in a healthy way when I give those dreams to you. Please give me a heart for the things you want to be a part of my life.

Afterglow

I will see the wonder of my life right now. I will give each day to God as an offering and make the most of every moment.

Your Heart Will Follow

Trust in what you love, continue to do it, and
it will take you where you need to go.

NATALIE GOLDBERG

———— ❧ ————

When our lives are directed by immediate needs rather than eternal hope, we will become stuck, thrown, lost, or flat out exhausted. And when that happens, all we want is a super long nap. Four days long would be ideal, but if you'll settle for a few cat naps and some times of prayer, I believe you'll be ready for this next step.

Start moving forward. You might not feel motivated or ready, but if you've become complacent or disheartened, you can get the momentum going. Have you experienced loss in your life? Reflect on that void, and then ask God to fill it up with his healing and renewal. If your job is dissatisfying or is consuming your energy, make time to do things you love—they could very well lead you to greater purpose. Is the weight of the world on your shoulders lately? Ease up on watching the news and take a break from filling your mind with images and sound bytes. Calm your spirit and pray without distraction—feel God's peace. If you lack motivation, yet desire to make a lasting change, seek accountability with others and commit to lifting up that area of your life in prayer daily.

It isn't always easy to break loose during those times of

stagnation, but it is time to live life like never before. Your life matters, and this day in your life matters. Move forward today. A baby step or a big leap will send you on your way…and your heart will follow.

Shedding Light

- Move forward—stop being stuck. Complacency or bitterness will set in if you don't give yourself over to God's momentum.

- Figure out what you need accountability for in your life, so that you can make lasting change. Set up a system of checks and balances either with friends or with goals.

- Breathe calm into your life little by little.

Prayer

I'll follow you today, God. I'll make room for you. I'll stop rushing ahead with my expectations and demands because they only lead me to more frustration and life noise. Help me to listen for the still, small voice within. Where are you taking me today? That is what I will ask each morning. And then I and my heart will follow.

Afterglow

I will show God the void in my heart, so that he can fill it with light and love.

What You Keep, What You Give

*There is only one real deprivation, I decided
this morning, and that is not to be able to
give one's gifts to those one loves most.*

May Sarton

―――⚬―――

We each have numerous gifts that we are born with, grow into, or are presented with during our faith journey. But the reason we have opportunity, inclination, or ability is not to raise ourselves up or to push forth our personal goals. Those gifts, often uncovered over time and during trials, are meant to be given to others on behalf of God. What might be a few of your gifts? Hospitality, service, leadership, musical ability, influence, sensitivity, creativity, teaching, praying, caregiving? The list of possibilities is as unique as you are. When you are not sure what gifts you have to give, start with the one we all have access to—a willing spirit. From that one gift, you can affect change, influence others, extend a helping hand, or raise the spirits and circumstances of those in need.

When gifts are saved and stored, they will form an ever-growing wall between you and your purpose. But when used and shared, our gifts lead us to a greater understanding of God's heart and his intention for our lives.

Shedding Light

- Struggling to find your gifts? Ask others what they see in you. Take the risk of unraveling the mystery of who you are.

- Have you been storing up your talents…saving them for a moment of great success? Start using those in ways that grow the servant in you. You'll discover how multifaceted those talents are and how they grow exponentially when they are shared.

Prayer

God, fill me with a sense of confidence and strength. When I try to hide behind my wall of insecurities, push me forward through the open gate of your will. When will I start trusting you with my life? All this time of faith, and yet I often move through my days like someone who doesn't know the mercy and might of the Creator. Show me those gifts and talents within me. Then show me how to start giving them away.

Afterglow

I won't "save my best" for later or for any purpose outside of serving others and God.

Expect More

*Don't live down to expectations. Go out
there and do something remarkable.*

WENDY WASSERSTEIN

Responsibilities can be overwhelming, but let's face it…there are many obligations and privileges that come with being part of a family or the human race for that matter. I have friends who are simultaneously managing the needs of their children and those of their elderly parents. Some things we sign on for— some are part of the life cycle.

Do you ever feel like you're living for someone else? That you've taken on someone else's expectations for your life? Expectations are different than responsibilities. When expectations are shaping your motivation for the day, they can turn your life inside out as you try to please someone other than God and live a life that isn't true to your purpose or calling.

If the expectations placed on you by others don't resonate as true for you or your happiness, start declaring your own. Life is way too short to have it dictated by guilt and guilt-based decisions. I don't mean that you pack your bag and head for the hills (you still have those responsibilities). Instead search your heart, seek God's leading, and find the direction that is your very own. Wouldn't it be great to live *for* God as God intended? Go do something remarkable! What are you waiting for?

Shedding Light

- If others have low expectations of you, step away from those limits and those deceptions.

- If you've bought into the need to maintain a high level of success, no matter the cost, then this is a destructive expectation that needs attention.

- Teach your children and others what life and living look like when grace replaces guilt.

Prayer

Guilt. I know it is not of you, God. It never has been. I used to rely on conviction that did come from you...and that gently guided me in the right direction, toward big love and sweet mercy. But then I started listening to guilt and the expectations of others. I should've known that being bullied into righteousness was not your will. Reveal to me the leading of the Spirit and allow me to hear and follow your voice only.

Afterglow

No more listening to guilt and expectations in stereo. I'll turn up the tune of grace and hum along.

You'll Be Filled

Honor yourself, the truth of who you are. In so doing,
develop yourself fully mind, body, and spirit. Always
offer your service without measure. It will fill you up.

BARBARA HARRIS, EDITOR-IN-CHIEF, *SHAPE* MAGAZINE

Inhale and exhale. Take a moment for peace and reflection. There's plenty more busyness to come, so do this for yourself freely. It is time to replenish that which seeps from your being, bit by bit, during days filled with worry, fear, second-guessing, performing, and juggling the impossible. What do you need restored today? We can start with hope. It is easy to lose it when we've been let down. God hasn't let you down. Now for a little grace. No…make that a lot. This has been with you all along, but you've forgotten to rest in God's grace because you've been so strong and determined.

What else has been emptied from your soul? Truth. Author Madeleine L'Engle wrote, "Truth is eternal, knowledge is changeable. It is disastrous to confuse them." As knowledge shifts, stand on the secure ground of truth. It will hold you. Peace always sounds so good. I think we believe it is intended for other people, those who don't live in the chaos we do. *Maybe peace is for those who sit on mountaintops and chant,* we think. Say the word *peace* over and over until it becomes a prayer and a reality. It is intended for you. Love is in God's presence. We can turn love into an obligation, but God reminds us that it is a gift. If you don't "feel the love," extend love first. It is okay to give and keep giving as God directs. He will fill you with what you need.

Shedding Light

- Have you mistaken changeable knowledge for permanent truth? Don't confuse the two. Grow in knowledge, and rest in truth.

- Is peace a stabilizing force in your life? Or is it still elusive. Study peace, sit with it, pray for it, and make it a daily practice. God's peace is yet another truth you can rest in.

Prayer

Give me your peace. Show me whatever things or people I use as a source of comfort instead of your peace. Help me stand in your peace, so that it is my truth and my reality even as trials come and go, even in the face of questions about faith, and even when life is going along smoothly, and I'm tempted to take credit.

Afterglow

I will spend time in meditation and be led to the peace of Christ.

Light a
Candle for
Transformation

A Little Praise

That is why I can never stop praising you;
I declare your glory all day long.

PSALM 71:8

A few words of praise can give us a sense of well-being, connection, and joy. A few words of praise can change our mood, shift our direction, and recreate our day. A few words of praise will transport us from the lowest depths to the highest heights. A few words of praise can remove the obstacles of hate and envy and free our way to love and compassion. A few words of praise lift the veil of human weakness and expose divine strength.

When words of praise are spoken, we are humbled and given insight into the might of God. Praise does more to brighten a life than any positive thinking or 15 seconds of fame ever could. Words of praise turn our slow walk into a happy gait. And when praise is given, we are reminded of the value and privilege of being a child of God.

When a few words of praise are spoken, we understand why there is nothing that we can't accomplish in God's power and will. All this goodness comes from a few words of praise…a few words of praise lifted up to our Creator.

Shedding Light

- Do you spend time praising God during the day? If not, why is this absent from your faith life?

- Speaking praises honors God and reminds you that he is the source of all life.

- Once you start praising God, you'll find that you are better equipped to praise the people in your life freely because your identity and worth no longer depend on gaining credit in the world's eyes.

Prayer

God, thank you for entering into a relationship with me. I'm just me, and you are the Founder and Creator of the world. How wonderful you are and how faithful. I have relied on your guiding hand to find my way. And when weary, I have fallen into your embrace time after time. I will praise you today for you are worthy.

Afterglow

I will praise God this morning, this afternoon, and this evening. And tomorrow I will do it again.

Awaiting Transformation

*What counts is whether we have been
transformed into a new creation. May God's
peace and mercy be upon all who live by this
principle; they are the new people of God.*

GALATIANS 6:15-16

A restless spirit can cause us to question what we are doing and why we're doing it. Have you experienced that kind of inner agitation and not sure why? Restlessness can creep upon us when life is going along as planned. It can emerge when we're in between milestones and living life in a holding pattern. The restlessness can feel like crisis to some and like awakening to others.

When a hunger arises or uncertainties flood your normally steadfast thoughts, you might be inclined to doubt everything, but it is the perfect time to believe—to believe in what God is preparing in your heart and spirit. Those stirrings are possibly the birthing pains of wonder and growth. God is preparing you for a trial, a change, an epiphany, a ministry, or a deeper level of faith. Sit with the uneasiness and the anticipation. During this time of awareness pray for direction, thank God for the unknown, and prepare to experience life and faith differently. View the shift in your spirit as a gift, even if it is uncomfortable.

More unsure about life than ever before? Welcome to the beginning of your transformation.

Shedding Light

- What triggers your uneasiness? What do you usually do to avoid exploring the root of it?

- Consider journaling through the uneasiness to see what is on the other side.

- Awakenings are not just for other people!

Prayer

I feel as though my soul is pacing as it waits for something new, something meaningful to take shape. I've felt this before, but I've tried to ignore it by revving up my external activity. I don't want to be afraid of hunger and longing because they lead me to you. Direct me and my next steps.

Afterglow

I will let hunger lead me back to God for answers.

Counseling Session One

*Why am I discouraged? Why is my heart
so sad? I will put my hope in God!*

PSALM 42:5

Sometimes what we need is an impromptu counseling session with no time to practice responses. Let's jump right into it and see what happens.

Imaginary Counselor: Tell me about it.

You: I made a big mistake, and I can't let go of it.

IC: You're human. Did you let go of it and give it to God?

You: Yes, but the guilt is strong, and I can't make it right. Why can't I fix this?

IC: God knows something that might help. I know it too. Ready?

You: Yes. But did I mention it was a big mistake?

IC: Here it is. You're human. Just as you need to know that God is bigger than your sin and he loves you unconditionally—you *also* have to recognize and admit that you are human. You can't fix this. God can.

You: I hurt others though. God must see that.

IC: He sees that you're human. And he sees that you need him. That's how it works.

You: I do need him.

IC: And?

You: My guilt won't make this right, only his grace does. I'm human and totally dependent on God to transform my sin into something resembling life and hope.

IC: Now, we're getting somewhere.

Shedding Light

- Speak to God directly, without practicing your responses. Discover what matters weigh heavy on your heart.

- How do you show God that you need him? Do others in your life see that you depend on God?

Prayer

Forgive me for the times that I hurt others knowingly and unknowingly. When I am holding onto my life and my sin, help me release these to your power and grace. I want to live a transformed life. I pray to see my meek offerings turned into evidences of hope through your love.

Afterglow

I'll accept that I'm human and express thanksgiving that God is the one who transforms my life.

Willing to Dream

Every great dream begins with a dreamer.
Always remember, you have within you the
strength, the patience, and the passion to
reach for the stars to change the world.

HARRIET TUBMAN

———— ∞ ————

What do you want to change about your world? When your heart breaks because there is so much pain and suffering, have you forgotten that you are here to make a difference? I shake my head at the problems around me. I even take these concerns to God in prayer. But I know that because I am God's child, I am to do more than notice those who hurt. When I see injustice and judgment where only grace could possibly heal, I can be that giver of grace.

Ask God to change your dreams into his own. It's a big request, and many of us are afraid to state it for the record. What if we don't know how to right a wrong or heal a heart wound? What if our capacity to love the unlovable is too limited? What if this step disrupts the life to which we have grown accustomed? If these doubts expressed as questions hold you back from asking God to give you his dreams for your life, then ask God for his heart first. It is tender and willing and open. Ask God for his eyes. They see others clearly, they envision the big picture, and they witness the hurting world.

God does not tire of answering questions or of giving. But as he gives, he is waiting for your "yes." He wants to give you a dream that will transform your life.

Shedding Light

- Will you replace your dream with God's dream for you?

- Seek ways to extend grace, to celebrate goodness, and to build up the hope in others.

- Be a healer and a dreamer. Live in God's truth, speak words of kindness, and reach out with actions of compassion.

Prayer

I want to be a big dreamer who is willing to leap into a life so much bigger, deeper, greater, and more significant than I could ever imagine. This abundant life is the one you have mapped out for me. You direct my steps and you prompt my heart.

Afterglow

I will carry the dreams of my Abba Father in my heart and into my tomorrow.

Counseling Session Two

*We must move from asking God to take care of
the things that are breaking our hearts, to praying
about the things that are breaking His heart.*

MARGARET GIBB

I think we got somewhere in the first session. Let's go back
in for another. It seems like there is something else you'd
like to address. Feel free.

Imaginary Counselor: Anything from last session that was
 helpful?

You: I know that I'm a human who makes mistakes and
 needs God.

IC: Excellent. What's been happening?

You: I feel lighter. God has transformed me and the former
 situation. It's too bad this awareness is trumped by a
 recent, unfortunate event.

IC: What happened?

You: Someone hurt me deeply. I can't get past it, and I
 don't think I ever will.

IC: So you didn't give the situation or the person over to
 God?

You: I tried, but that doesn't change how I feel about this
 person now.

IC: God knows something that might help. I know it too.
 Ready?

You: Yes. Did I mention that I was deeply hurt and broken-hearted?

IC: Here it is. That person who hurt you is human. Just as you need to know that God is bigger than their sin and he loves them unconditionally—you *also* have to recognize and admit that other people are human. You can't fix this. God can.

You: That sounds familiar.

IC: The truths about God's love and forgiveness that transform your life are also available to others. Don't just pray for your life to go smoothly. Pray for that other person and their wholeness. But that will mean that you...

You: I know…I'll need God to do this, right?

IC: Absolutely.

Shedding Light

- What have you been trying to fix on your own and in your own power? Ready, set, let go.

- The intimate, personal, transforming lessons of faith that you learn are also lessons about how God relates to others.

- Remember that the person you are struggling with is a person who is broken, just like you. Pray for their wholeness as well as your own.

Prayer

God, I give you my heart and I give you my struggles with others. You know what is at stake in each relationship. You see where I am hardened. You watch me push buttons instead of embrace grace. Sometimes I think I hold onto my hurts because I don't want to admit my own transgressions. Transform this stubborn heart of mine, God.

Afterglow

I'll apply what I learn about God's transforming power to my life and relationships with other fallible humans.

Light a Candle
for Grace

Taking Notes

In grief, one can endure the day, just the day. But when one also tries to bear the grief ahead, one cannot compass it. As for happiness, it can only be the ability to experience the moment. It is not next year that life will be so flawless and if we keep trying to wait for next year's happiness, the river of time will wind past and we shall not have lived at all.

GLADYS TABER, *STILLMEADOW DAY BOOK*

I mourn the fact that I've done very little journaling during the past couple of years. Many index cards bearing notes or quotes are crumpled in the bottom of my numerous purses and backpacks. But I feel the loss of not having a coherent gathering of my recollections because I've journeyed through a great trial and have learned about healing and mercy.

I imagine there are seasons when you are observing life, taking note of every drop of wisdom that comes to you, and sitting like a pupil eager to jot down God's truths as they are presented. You've probably also discovered, as I have, that there are seasons when we are called to invest every bit of ourselves into the living—when we cannot fully reflect on life as it is passing, or we will certainly miss being present for what God is teaching us. And do not be mistaken—these times of great work, grief, loss, perseverance, and endurance are teaching us about living and faithfulness.

I've missed having the time and distance to process my faith journey. God has pulled me out of my comfort zone and into full, immediate, sometimes difficult, and always abundant living. The big lessons often emerge amidst a cyclone when there is no time to make sense of them during the experience. But if we are faithful and persevere in God's strength, those lessons are not lost in the uncertainty of a storm, for these God-lessons have been impressed upon our hearts to carry with us wherever the path leads.

Shedding Light

- Is this a time to do more observing and reflecting? Or is it a time to press on in life...fully focused on the living? Maybe you are at that place of balance. No matter the season...stay connected to God and his voice.

- What certainty, learned during an earlier time of chaos or pain, do you carry today?

Prayer

God, help me to understand the lessons I am to learn during this time. Help me to stand on the wonderful truths I've learned from my past trials. When the winds of change have rushed through my life, and I felt so out of control, you were the ever-present sense of peace. Carry me today as you did then. May I always praise you for your grace.

Afterglow

I will allow eternal impressions to be made on my heart today, so that truth travels with me and changes me.

Landscape of Grace

*What would a sinless life look like? I can
only imagine. Strive as I may, I won't achieve
it. My interior landscape is scarred.*

CINDY CROSBY

Our eyes grow accustomed to the view from where we stand
in life. The streets and intersections are known by heart.
We can greet by name many of the people we encounter. Even
the people we don't know have familiar faces, and we can nod
to them. We know the best route to our favorite stores, and
we slip into "our" spot at church, at work, and at our corner
coffee shop. This view is consistent. Comfortable. And frankly
it's one we could experience with our eyes closed.

We always need grace. But when we turn to its power with
desperation and heart, our view tends to have shifted from the
known to the unknown. We don't recognize the path, and there
is little comfort found as we maneuver the unfamiliar. But there
is grace. It opens our eyes to God's presence and his involvement
with our lives. In times of sickness, healing rises. In seasons of
despair, hope emerges. In days of fear, peace materializes. In
moments of doubt, faith appears.

Be thankful to have your eyes opened to the landscape of
grace—it is as vast as the unknown. But in a life dependent on
God, it becomes as familiar as the terrain of our own hearts.

Shedding Light

- View the unfamiliar terrain as a good thing—an opportunity to shift from independence to total dependence on God.

- Change up your routine. You don't have to wait for a life change or trial to awaken to the landscape of grace. Step out more. Talk to new people. Take a risk by being vulnerable.

- Comfort is something to be grateful for. But getting too comfortable in life can undermine a sense of gratitude.

Prayer

Open my eyes to what I am supposed to see.
Open my eyes to what I am supposed to be.
Open my eyes to see the ache in the person before me.
Open my eyes to see the need in this culture of plenty.
Open my eyes to witness healing in the middle of pain.
Open my eyes to see the warm glow of grace cast against
     the shadow of my complacency.

Afterglow

Today I'll resist the temptation to keep life predictable and experience the renewal of grace.

Falling Apart

*This thing that we call "failure" is not the
falling down, but the staying down.*

MARY PICKFORD

A huge bill arrives in the mail when you're financially
tapped out. The kids are stuck in whine mode. You get
one more serving of bad news than you can digest. Pressure at
work and at home makes it impossible to pretend everything
is fine. Or maybe you have one day filled with a series of mis-
fortunate events that leaves you floored and unsure how to get
back up.

Why is it that "pick yourself up and dust yourself off"
sounds like encouragement when we're saying it to a five-
year-old, but when we say it to ourselves, it sounds unfeeling,
even cruel? First of all you aren't hurting because someone is
in your favorite swing. Second "pick yourself up" outlives its
effectiveness after about 20 times. But having faith means you
have more than clichés for consolation—you have God's comfort and strength to get you back on your feet.

A friend and I contemplated what life would be like if we
rarely experienced "failure" or circumstances that knocked us
over. We wouldn't rely on God's mercy and power. We wouldn't
know the wonder of grace or gratitude. And we wouldn't have

the sweet assurance that when life is hard, we haven't fallen from grace—we're being carried by it.

Shedding Light

- What does grace mean to you? How does God's grace impact your life and how you view your trials?

- Have you told yourself to "pick yourself up" so many times that it feels unkind? Be gentle with yourself when you struggle. Go to God. He'll give you strength along with kind, helpful words.

Prayer

God, lift me up out of this circumstance. I feel tired and useless. I'm such a pro at grinning and bearing it that I've forgotten how to process my emotions when something does go wrong. I want to feel the struggle only so that I can bring it to you honestly. I won't hide bits of it from myself or you so that I appear stronger. I want to lean into your strength and be carried by grace.

Afterglow

Tough days are nothing new. But how I treat them and myself during the tough days will be a new thing.

A New Direction

I do not at all understand the mystery of grace—only that it meets us where we are but does not leave us where it found us.

ANNE LAMOTT

———— ✦ ————

I saw a young boy pacing in front of a driveway while he waited impatiently for his parents to finish talking with friends. The last time I saw pacing was in a 1950's comedy where the husband robotically walked the width of a maternity ward hallway. The thing about walking back and forth is that you don't get anywhere, no matter how many times you do it (just ask the boy).

When we are pacing, trying to find our way out of a box created by sin, frailty, pride, lack of wisdom, or any number of things, it is only God and his grace that can get us out of this futile pattern. His grace covers us and transforms us. It does not leave us to walk into a wall, turn around, and start all over again…it leads us beyond the limits of our sin and humanity and allows us to walk in God's freedom.

When we are going nowhere, God's grace changes that. He does not leave us where he finds us. He gives us a new direction and the hope of healing, and he sets us in motion…going forward toward a future.

Shedding Light

- What is making you pace right now? Are you getting weary from this pattern of going nowhere? Go to God and ask for a new path through familiar troubles.

- Sins and lies and unhealthy relationships box us in. And when we try to correct these, on our own with human solutions, we're usually just building a slightly bigger box around the old one.

- Walking in God's freedom will feel different. You'll discover a life without limits.

Prayer

God, I walk back and forth carrying my broken pieces. I show them to others and we take notes about the brokenness. I add pieces to the pile because I tell myself there's no time to place them in your hands. No wonder I'm overwhelmed... I'm saving and transporting the very pieces you have asked me to surrender. I'm ready to give these up. I might not like it at first. What will I do when I don't have to tend to my brokenness day in and day out?

Afterglow

I plan to discover what it feels like to be unburdened. I plan to live in grace.

A Brave Grace

Courage is fear that has said its prayers.

Dorothy Bernard

—————❧—————

Life requires courageous steps, big and small. Sometimes just getting out of bed is an act of bravery. Following God's leading when it is outside of our expectations or plans is an act of courage. Trusting God's forgiveness when we feel unworthy is an act of courage. And that kind of courage is ours only when we depend on God through and in spite of our fears. Such strength becomes a part of our character when we face a conflict, a need, or an average day head-on with prayer. When we can look at our lives as an offering, a sacrifice to God, then we are acting with fierce faith.

"Saying grace" seems an old-fashioned term for prayer. Rarely do you hear this particular phrase mentioned at a dining table where pizza is served and those gathering around are 15 minutes late to soccer practice or eager to get back to their computer games. But saying grace is a way to introduce our side of grace—giving thanks. Bring the act of giving thanks back into your life and the lives of your family members. It will lead them to greater faith. It will lead them to gratitude. It will lead them to courage.

Shedding Light

- Why do you feel unworthy? Sometimes the thing or the person or the event that initially caused us to feel unworthy is not even something in our present life. We've just been afraid to believe in something better.

- How are you strong? In what ways do you exhibit strength and truth in your life?

- Spend time giving thanks for your recent joys, the latest problems, and those past happenings that gave root to bitterness. These all are meant to lead you to God. What could give us more gratitude than that?

Prayer

I've spent a lot of time dwelling on my fears. Even though I know you and your peace, I turn back to the way of fear. Lead me through these times. When simple worries morph into a foundation of fear, I will return to the courage I have in you. I need not tremble. I need not avoid living. Thank you for every circumstance that turns my thoughts back to you and my heart toward you.

Afterglow

I'll embrace courage as a God-given character trait, and I will give thanks!

Light a Candle
for Sanctuary

Shaping Space for God

As I started looking, I found more and more.

VALERIE STEELE

———— ✧ ————

In a magazine interview, singer Dolly Parton mentioned that, on all of her properties, she has either a chapel or an area with a *prie dieu* kneeler, so that she can take time for prayer and silence during a busy life. I loved this idea, and it reminded me of some of my past goals related to making room for God and prayer. For some time I have wanted to create a space in my home for this very thing, but I have put it off. For some time I have wanted to discipline myself to read and reflect on Scripture and journal my responses to it, but I have put it off.

When life throws obstacles in our way or troubles arise, we do not hesitate to seek God immediately. We ask for a meeting right then and there. Wouldn't it be so much better if we had an ongoing session scheduled with God all ready? Wouldn't it be great if we gave our hearts and minds and lives over to God daily and felt that immediate sense of his presence no matter what our circumstances?

Don't put off making space for God in your life. Set aside a very deliberate, special, meaningful portion of your day, your heart, and your home and dedicate them to God. The more you seek God throughout your day, the more intimately you'll know God.

Shedding Light

- Prepare a place of prayer in your life. Make this a meaningful space. Maybe that comfy chair that only gets used when company comes over can be placed near a window for your special spot. Maybe your sanctuary is a walking path along a river. You don't have to sit to meditate and pray.

- Go back to the tried and true Sunday school practice of memorizing verses. Rest in the comfort, inspiration, and peace they offer...that God offers.

Prayer

Give me a heart that seeks the refuge of your love automatically. Whether I'm making decisions, facing sickness or struggle, or walking an unplanned course...I will start my journey in your sanctuary. I will praise you as I enter your presence, and I will listen for your leading.

Afterglow

I will connect with God more frequently, so that the path to his presence becomes familiar to my heart and soul.

An Unfolding Mystery

In all that I value, there is a core of mystery.

MARGE PIERCY

There is mystery tied to faith. That can scare some. It can intimidate others. But if you consider for one moment how incredibly refreshing it is to not know all the answers, you'll understand the allure of deep faith. In an age when we can look up a definition, a history, a ten-year plan for almost anything and everything via the internet, we should embrace the idea of faith. Faith influences our lives. It defines us. It leads us through days that would, without faith, make us drop to our knees in defeat.

As much as we study, research, pick apart, and analyze faith, it still beholds the beauty of mystery. This is such a lovely part of belief, and yet we want to feel "in the know" and in control of the information that relates to what we base our life on. That is understandable, but our desire for absolutes undermines the wonder of miracles, and it steals the joy that could be ours for holding onto belief even when we *don't* know all the answers.

Celebrate the unknowns of faith. If we could pinpoint every single truth of faith, it might make us sought-out scholars, but it would do little to build up our hope in the Lord. The world holds such little potential for mystery and wonder. We are the privileged few—those of us who cling to hope not only in spite of the questions but because of them.

Shedding Light

- Have you ever thought about how freeing it is to *not* know all the answers? Spend time praying about this newly recognized freedom. How might your daily life change once you rest in this freedom?

- When you share faith with others, take time to step away from theology and debate and describe the intimate beauty of faith that you have personally experienced.

Prayer

Lead me to wonder. When I try to define you and your love, let me rest with the same assurance in the aspects of you and your nature that I can and cannot define. Thank you for delighting me with surprises that take my breath away and reminding me of the miracle of life and the wonders of how you work in and through circumstances and people.

Afterglow

I will live as a person who believes in miracles and who honors the mystery of faith.

Passport

Send out your light and your truth;
let them guide me.

PSALM 43:3

What transports you to a sanctuary mind-set? A friend of mine who loves to travel was feeling a strong pull to return to Europe. I had been craving the same. Since her life was incredibly busy and a quick jaunt to another country was hardly feasible, she decided to go to a local coffeehouse, order a cappuccino in a mug, and sit at a table for a few minutes. Not quite a Parisian vacation, and yet it was her passport to happiness. A couple weeks later, she and I enjoyed several cappuccinos together in similar fashion. It led us both back to the fun and camaraderie of our original trip. I was grateful for the opportunity.

Is there a time or place you think of that fills you with joy? Is there a way for you to recapture that same feeling? I find that when I look at photos of a happy moment in my life or of someone that I care about, I smile, relax, and settle into contentment. When I revisit a favorite book during a rare, leisurely afternoon, I am refreshed and satisfied. We forget to take time for important moments of peace, reflection, and joy.

If you've struggled to create a practice of daily meditation and devotion, find ways to recapture the joy of spending time with God. A few moments in prayer will transport you to God's presence. You'll be grateful for the opportunity.

Shedding Light

- When was the last time you experienced pure joy? Can you duplicate this or recreate it in a new form today?

- Prayer can be a passport out of regret and into the land of peace. It can transport you from a time of self-focus to a place of compassion. Prayer changes your heart and where you stand in faith.

Prayer

Take me away from the monotony of today. I barely can distinguish today from yesterday or the week before. I want to savor these moments of family, interaction, new challenges, and living. God, help me watch for the joy that can grace even the most routine day. Lead me to people who readily share joy and direct my spirit and mind-set to receive happiness like manna from heaven.

Afterglow

I will retrace my steps to a place of happiness. God is there, and he'll help me bring forth the joy in my life.

Spiritual Garden Sanctuary

*The greatest gift of the garden is the
restoration of the five senses.*

HANNA RION

———— ∽ ————

Having a sanctuary to go to is a gift. There is a hilltop garden in my town. When spring comes around each year, this is a tranquil place to wander along pea gravel paths under a canopy of vibrantly colored flowers and shade-giving foliage. Many caring hands and hearts have worked to create such a sacred space, and I am blessed to reap the benefits. At the crest of the hill is a lookout. From here the busyness of life fades to the background and the beauty of life comes to the forefront.

A heart that is given over to God becomes a sanctuary that, no matter the season, provides a tranquil refuge. Such a sacred space can be created when we allow moments of stillness to become intentional sessions of prayer and reflection, not fleeting intermissions. When we evaluate our lives and weed out the chaos so that peace and meaning can grow, we are tending to this inner garden. And when we choose to walk alongside God rather than rush past him with our own agendas and routes, we will see the sights he intends for us to experience.

Take time to revel in reverence and awe of God's goodness here in the spiritual sanctuary of your heart. Here the busyness of life fades to the background, and the beauty of life comes to the forefront…and you are richly blessed as your senses awaken.

Shedding Light

- Quiet is not absence. Stillness is not inaction. Sanctuary is not escape.

- Invite God's goodness to infuse your existence. Only then can you know it intimately. Only then can you share it.

- Even if you don't run around with your every move planned, chances are you live by your own agenda. Try to give that over to God this week. Leave space for what God might be offering you. It might be rest, a conversation, an idea, a prayer. God only knows!

Prayer

I don't always see the weeds that crop up in my habits and plans. God, point out those activities, thoughts, and expectations that don't belong in the sanctuary you've planned for me. Give me the discipline and discernment to rid my life of them. I want to make room for the flowers of hope and potential you plant alongside my journey's road.

Afterglow

I am a blessed child of God. I'll walk forward in this identity rather than one shaped by my success, performance, or goals.

So Good

Taste and see that the LORD is good. Oh, the
joys of those who take refuge in him!

PSALM 34:8

It's so good to be here, in this place of refuge. This is the heart of God. Some might mistakenly see God's refuge as a barrier that separates us from the world. They might want it to become a protective wall between our hearts and the harsh times of doubt. But those scenarios aren't examples of godly refuge, they're illustrations of separation and confinement.

God's refuge is a garden with plenty of benches on which to sit and think and pray. God's refuge is an open field where we can walk for miles safely and happily, even when storm clouds rumble above. God's refuge is a gentle valley where we can climb to the top of a hill at night and watch the stars with pure joy and wonder.

I don't think God's refuge has a lot of posted rules. I think that when we are here in it, when our hearts are longing for communion with God, we are gently nudged in the right directions and lovingly taught the things of goodness and meaning. We see paths with greater understanding, discernment, and clarity. And we see the needs and hearts of others with less judgment and more compassion.

How do you know when you are in God's presence? By the heightened awareness of what is good and life-giving.

Shedding Light

- Did you grow up with a lot of rules and very little gentle guidance? It can be difficult to discern the voice of God when we have not known the voice of love in our human relationships. Consider studying the ways of God's love during your time of meditation.

- Has there been a time when you used the idea of refuge to close yourself off from the world? If you are still there, find a way beyond this self-prescribed gated community. Start living a life of faith out where it can have influence and effect.

Prayer

I'll run and run and never reach the limits of your love. I'll stare at the sky throughout the night and never see its edges. There is comfort in the limitless expanse of your love and compassion. Teach me to breathe deeply and rest in this freedom. May I recognize that which is pure and noble and good in this life.

Afterglow

With the goal of freedom, I will tear down this protective wall that I built or that others built for me.

The Way of the Heart

*I wonder sometimes if we haven't banished the way
of the heart in favor of the way of the mind, if we
emphasize learning about God over being with God.*

SUE MONK KIDD, *WHEN THE HEART WAITS*

Light a candle. Watch the flame. Don't force yourself into thoughts or pressure yourself to come up with the right words to say. When your heart wants to create an offering of a simple prayer, your mind mentions that God created Kilimanjaro and gravity and all of a sudden…those words about hope and thanksgiving seem meager and insignificant. When your heart is ready to share its brokenness, your mind weighs the labor involved in healing and wholeness, and you second-guess embarking on the journey. How often do we get in our own way of sweet communion with God?

But when you enter God's presence, you'll feel comforted rather than burdened by the mystery of the unknown. You'll be able to let go of the loud inner-judge and give way to God's grace and acceptance. But you have to leave the way of the world, the way of control and preconceived notions, at the door of your sanctuary, whether it is a church, a room, or your heart.

Just for once (or even better, try it as a regular habit) let go of your head knowledge of prayer and God. That knowledge is important, and useful, and builds your foundation to faith…but right now, in this moment, let your heart take over. It has amazing things to share with its Creator. And it will lead you to sanctuary.

Shedding Light

- Let your heart speak. What does it want to say to God? What has prevented you from allowing your heart to speak honestly in the past?
- When you are with God…be with him fully, wholly, and with an open heart and spirit.

Prayer

God, my heart is ready to express its love, its hurts, and its longings. My mind is ready to quit overriding what my heart wants to share and receive. I'm made to have intimacy with you. Thank you for preparing in me that desire for communication and for the peace that comes only from your heart. The gift of sanctuary permeates my life. All I want is to be with you.

Afterglow

I will make prayer a priority. I will follow the way of the heart straight to God's presence.

Light a Candle
for Connection

Potluck Faith

*Who is greater, the one who is at the table or the
one who serves? Is it not the one who is at the
table? But I am among you as one who serves.*

LUKE 22:27 NIV

I've had a strange, recurring idea lately. It involves clearing
away the living room furniture to make room for a cluster of tables. It requires the act of inviting people from different subgroups in my life to enter our home and share a meal
or two or three. This vision is especially crazy because I don't
cook. It's a bit uncomfortable because, as a personal rule of
thumb, I prefer solitary experiences over group ones. And it's
risky because I don't know who would show up and what the
event would be like.

What do you do with random "potluck" ideas that tug at
your heart? Are you someone who finds change difficult, even
when it seems to be God's leading? Numerous times I've resisted
the convictions of the heart. With my 20/20 hindsight, I see
how those were missed opportunities to grow and to inspire
others to grow.

Is God leading you toward connection with others in new
ways? How would following this call expand your life, enrich
it, complicate it, rescue it? When we say yes to opening up our
hearts, we often don't know what we'll get, but we do know

of a few certainties: We will discover new things about ourselves, others, and God's nature. We will be restless and even frustrated about changing the way we do things. And we will be scared. These are also the very reasons to join the mismatch gathering of hungry folks at God's table. You will fill up on strength, mercy, and wisdom…and you will be asked to share this feast with others.

Shedding Light

- How are you called to serve others or to create community? What keeps you from following this leading? Follow through with small ways to be more inclusive and to share your life.

- What are some of the most absurd ideas you wish you had followed through on in your past?

- What opportunity is rising up in your life right now that you want to embrace?

Prayer

God, lead my heart toward the uncomfortable ways of growth and the remarkable ways of hospitality. Rid me of my expectations and my desire to control the outcome so that I can overflow with your love. May I see every person as your child.

Afterglow

Today I will light a candle and enter God's presence. I will sit at his table, eager to be filled with his love and compassion for others.

Leaning into God

Truly, it is in the darkness that one finds the light,
so when we are in sorrow, then this
light is nearest of all to us.

MEISTER ECKHART

When we are feeling lonely, afraid, mildly anxious, or anything along the fear spectrum, we want connection with others. But we don't always know how to make that happen. I think the more isolated we are in our emotional state, the more we tend to wait for others to break through to us, to understand our emotional need or crisis, and to rescue us.

However, what we need to do is to reach out past our hurt or malaise and connect with others on our own initiative. It isn't easy to be vulnerable and open, is it? We learn to hold back those things that are unsettling or that might raise an eyebrow if expressed in certain "speak only of good things" company. Many of us have the same problem in our relationship with God. Instead of going to him with our needs, we wait for a thundering message to waken us from depression or an unbelievably great job offer to be extended to us by a stranger we meet in a Starbucks line. Those fantasies aren't nearly as powerful as our act of reaching out to God in our pain or need.

We'll learn how to receive help when we're willing to be vulnerable enough to share that need. There will be times when a discerning, prayerful friend shows up just when we need her. And there will be times when a conversation with a stranger does lead to something amazing. God acts on our behalf all the time. Leaning into his strength and leaning on his provision becomes our nature if we give ourselves to him openly and honestly each day (emotional mess days included). From those Mondays when we don't want to get out of bed to the days when a great loss leaves us unable to catch our breath…our first action only needs to be a conversation with God.

Shedding Light

- Is your pattern to wait for help instead of asking for it? Try to be more vulnerable in your communication with others, including God. Express your doubts and your needs, especially in prayer.

- Did you ever do a "trust fall" at camp or school? A person stands behind you and you fall back, trusting them to catch you. This is a great visual to have in mind when you pray. Imagine falling back as God catches you and your circumstance every time.

Prayer

I'm learning to be more open about my heartache and hopes. When I lean into your understanding and strength, I know you catch me each time. God, help me to trust more.

Afterglow

Today I will move toward vulnerability with someone I know. And tonight I will pray openly. I will confess my need for God.

Learning a New Language

If we use no ceremony toward others,
we shall be treated without any.

WILLIAM HAZLITT

———————⌗———————

To become fluent in a language, you not only learn vocabulary words and verb conjugations, you also study conversational customs and rhythm. When talking to a stranger or a business proprietor, Spanish speakers initiate conversation by making a personal connection. They ask how the other person is doing, and they wait for responses from the other person. These inquiries are not only pleasantries, but also extensions of respect, courtesy, and kindness. They are invitations to connect.

When I think of how task focused I have become in my interactions, it's a bit shameful. My mind usually skips past pleasantries and goes straight to an objective. I have many excuses: I feel scattered or forgetful much of the time, and I don't want to lose my train of thought (have you ever tried to stop a moving train?). Also, I'm a prime representative of a culture that is self-focused, in a hurry, and disconnected. My false sense of urgency overrides the need to connect with others at a personal, heart level. The problem is…I'm missing out on a lot of the dialogue of life.

To engage in true dialogue with another requires that we first offer up a bit of ourselves and then invite others to join the conversation. That can often be a scary, vulnerable, or time-consuming choice, but it is the most direct way to speak heart-to-heart with another. When we stop talking *at* others and start sharing *with* them, we achieve a deeper connection.

If you desire to become fluent in the language of faith, invite people to dialogue and stay long enough to learn a little something. Become an interpreter of the complex heart language. By all means, study your nouns and your verbs, but let us focus keenly on our adjectives: kind, caring, attentive, open, inviting, authentic.

Shedding Light

- Start a conversation with the intention of learning more about the other person or encouraging someone.

- The language of faith takes practice. Not so that it becomes rote, but so that it becomes authentic. Seek to be authentic in the words you choose and the way you respond to the comments of others. This will lead to deeper dialogue.

Prayer

God, let me speak to those I encounter with respect and consideration. Give me sensitivity to hear the needs of others, and give me patience to relate to and respond to what they aren't saying.

Afterglow

I'll make the effort to live out my verbs—love, listen, hear, accept, respond, believe, pray.

Add a Friend

Friendship marks a life even more deeply than love.

ELIE WIESEL

For the longest time I resisted joining online communities. Then, when a good friend moved away, she encouraged me to make the leap into the ether playground. For someone who prefers to keep her personal life personal, I was surprised to see benefits to this public display of connection.

And then I was asked to "add a friend."

In "real" life I've become reluctant to add new relationships to my circle. Each friendship requires nurturing and attention (a good one, anyway), so I'm cautious. And now I'm supposed to add a friend of a friend? Or the guy who has something in common with someone I went to high school with? Well, okay…because this is what the world of multiplying cyberships is all about. It's a bit like asking everyone in your fifth grade class to be your valentine. It was a general gesture of friendship, no strings attached.

And then someone sent me a cyber fish.

And a tree and a kiss and a painting and a flower. And would I like to return the favor by sending a fish, a tree, a kiss, a painting, a flower? Now these were starting to feel like real relationships, the kind that take energy and effort. The ones I reluctantly add to my life. Sigh. But I've decided that this rabbit trail party serves as a positive reminder that it can be enjoyable to "add a friend" without overthinking what's involved. Do you overthink friendships and pull back because of the responsibility?

Wouldn't God want us to "accept" rather than "decline" those people who do come into our lives daily? This is a lesson I'm still working on. Will you be my friend? I can promise you one thing…I'll never send you a fish.

Shedding Light

- Do you feel too limited by time and energy to pursue any more relationships? Try to welcome a new friendship into your life without evaluating it.

- What do you consider your community? How can you develop your connection to that community?

Prayer

Give me a desire to welcome new people into my life. I want to be able to accept others and share my life with them. When I want to build up my walls, my filters…remind me to remain open and generous with my time and my compassion.

Afterglow

I'll reach out to others more frequently. I'll engage in conversations and expand my community.

The Agenda of Authenticity

There is never any great achievement by the things of religion without a heart deeply affected by those things.

JONATHAN EDWARDS

Talking about beliefs that define us stirs up the emotions tied to those matters of significance. As it should be…we are passionate about anything that fuels our personal passions. But those emotions, so strong as they rise up, can overwhelm our message. If you have anything you want to present to others as true, as life-changing, or of importance to you…your primary agenda should be authenticity.

When we try to force a viewpoint, control conversations, or concoct situations so that we have a person "right where we want them," we sacrifice the chance to be a representative of our message and have settled for being a lobbyist. But a lobbyist, true to their moniker, always remains on the outside as they try to influence happenings on the inside.

Unfortunately, a lobbyist is left to rely on pressure and entice-ments as their bag of tricks. An emotional lobbyist is not able to enter the interior of a person's heart or circle of trust. Instead, become a representative for your important message. Share your heart; don't sell it. As you develop a relationship with another and witness what their needs are, then the door to their heart is open to receive you and to hear what matters to you. A lobbyist might gain power, but a representative gains understanding and credibility and the right to speak from their heart about those things that compel them. The bag full of tricks can be replaced with a heart that is full of truth, empathy, and compassion.

Shedding Light

- Are you trying to be a lobbyist for something you believe in? Stop forcing issues and start fueling relationships.

- The fastest way to become a representative is to become a listener. Practice listening in every situation. Stop offering up your solution at every lull in the conversation. Rest in the experience of getting to know someone. You will discover the best way to love that person.

Prayer

Lord, guide me to see what others bring to the table. When I think that I am always the teacher or the leader, I am sacrificing my chance to be a student. I want to see each new situation and each person I meet as an opportunity to learn more of your nature and your ways. Help me to rest in being a listener and a person who nurtures another's heart. This is how faith interacts with another. This is how compassion works.

Afterglow

I will toss aside my agenda so that I can catch a sense of compassion for others.

Strong Connection

*Only when one is connected to one's inner core is
one connected to others. And, for me, the core, the
inner spring, can best be re-found through solitude.*

ANNE MORROW LINDBERGH

"Give me my space!" Have you ever wanted to shout this to someone or pray it fervently to God after a long day? This might seem like the cry of a distant, indifferent person, but there is much value in the sacred act of creating space and resting in solitude. Not so that we can distance ourselves from community and covenant with others, but so that we can take time to restore our sense of peace and wellness as God's child.

When I take advantage of solitude to seek God's heart, I am renewing my sense of connection with every person on earth. When I light a candle and lift up the prayer that has gone unspoken for days because I've been too distracted or self-centered, I experience renewal, hope, and sensitivity toward others. We come to God with our weary hearts and our specific praises and petitions, and Abba graciously receives them and embraces us with assurances and peace. And then something wonderful happens within the very core of our spiritual self...we see beyond ourselves. We can walk among the masses and feel lonely, but as we enter God's presence, we are no longer isolated in our thoughts. We are given the security of his very real attention and love, and we are guided to notice that we are a part of something so much bigger than our current concern.

As much as I lean toward being a loner, I know this can never be my identity. Because as soon as I slip into God's presence and think on how interconnected my life is with that of the stranger I passed at the coffee shop or the best friend I've had since high school…I get chills. This is the body of Christ. I'm a part of it. You're a part of it.

Shedding Light

- Allow yourself time in solitude along with silence. After you read a devotion, allow another ten minutes to pass in which you assign no specific task other than to meet God.

- Does the idea of solitude make your palms sweat and your mind soar with ways to sabotage any blip of alone time? Each round does not have to be in silence. Choose good background music for your time alone. Bake something. Whistle. Journal. Just let your thoughts be of and for God.

Prayer

Calm the pace of my heartbeat. Steady my thoughts. Ready my spirit. I want to experience your presence, God.

Afterglow

I'll figure out how to dedicate some of my alone time to seeing and seeking God.

Light a Candle
for Clarity

I Can See Clearly Now

*Saul headed toward Damascus. As he
came near the city, a bright light from
heaven suddenly flashed around him.*

ACTS 9:3 NCV

A glimpse of light can trigger within us a sense of hope and peace. It can illuminate the very best in our hearts. The symbolic flame of a wedding unity candle indicating two lives joined as one. The bright eyes of a child discovering the world around them. An advent candle lit to mark the holy season. The silvery white of an ultrasound image outlining the miracle of new life.

The most powerful, the most moving, the most transforming light is that of God's love. That can sound like a phrase pulled from an overused religious dictionary, but when we encounter the brilliant purity of mercy, the cliché ends and the Christ experience begins.

I have a fondness for the exciting story of Saul's conversion on the road to Damascus. I don't find it overly dramatic or hard to embrace as truth. To me, it makes perfect sense that Saul, a persecutor of Christians and vehement hater of Christ, encountered his road to conversion, his path to faith, and his way to clarity with the help of a blinding light.

When God casts his light on our lives, the shadows are

exposed. We notice the dirt of sin, the smudges of bad judgment, and the wounds of our brokenness, and we realize how off course our lives have been. Then, in a flash of grace, those blemishes and regrets are washed away. Our new vision reveals the way to the hope, peace, and faith of a transformed life. We just have to walk forward.

Shedding Light

- What is God shedding light on in your life right now? How will this transform your faith from this day forward?

- Step out of the shadows that have darkened your life in the past. What will this freedom mean to you?

Prayer

God, your light guides me to ways and thoughts of peace. You've transformed me with grace, and you've illuminated my path of purpose. Help me live in the light so that my shadows are revealed, and I am able to live a transformed life. Amen.

Afterglow

I will walk forward in grace and will celebrate my encounter with God's love.

An Awakened Faith

*They have eyes to see but do not see and
ears to hear but do not hear.*

EZEKIEL 12:2 NIV

———— ∞ ————

When I get run down or overly stressed, a haze covers my thoughts and I react in slow motion. I lack control of my body. My arms and legs don't feel like my own. A friend will point to a big bruise and ask what happened, and I shrug my foggy "I dunno" shrug. More times than not, the bruise was formed when I walked into the rocking chair or hit my hand against the buffet in the dining room, both of which have been in the same locations for years.

Unfortunately, these times of weariness and emotional survival can cause more than a bruised knee. These times of internal processing and disconnect from my outer world cause me to be careless with my words, comments, and attitude. I stop watching for and listening for God's direction. I don't have the energy to care about what unfolds each day or who about me has needs. The social and spiritual filters I should use to determine when something I'm about to say is helpful or hurtful are defective. My careless responses and remarks can bruise the feelings of those in my path. I don't listen very patiently to my husband. I become more blunt than honest with friends. And my social graces all but disappear when I have to mix and mingle or just make it through the 15-items-or-less line.

When we are spiritually worn out or hard-hearted, we will also experience this time of wandering aimlessly, in a haze. We become careless with our hearts and our sense of truth, and we tend to run into obstacles more frequently. It is as important to find ways to stay spiritually alert as it is mentally alert. The way to health in both categories can be similar. Pray more/rest more. Get fed spiritually/eat healthily. Make time for fellowship/take time for friendships. Break away for spiritual reflection/give yourself a break. This will lead to your awakening.

Care more about this life you're walking through...it is physical *and* spiritual...and nothing less.

Shedding Light

- How has your spiritual and physical life shown signs of weariness?

- What has caused the most heart bruises in your life?

- How can you use this time of refreshment to restore clarity and hope? Why do you want to be "awake" in your faith and life?

Prayer

Remove this haze from my life, God. I want to be fully aware of each day and each opportunity to grow in my understanding of faith and hope. You provide rest for this weary child of yours. Thank you.

Afterglow

I will start each day with a focused prayer, asking for eyes to see and ears to hear. I don't want to miss the life God is showing me.

The Real Thing

Hold a true friend with both your hands.

NIGERIAN PROVERB

Like any relationship, a friendship can run on empty when one or both parties have to work too hard to keep it running. As we mature and discover more about ourselves, it can be important to evaluate the health of our friendships. Do some friends feed your soul, while others continually undermine your heart and purpose? Do some withhold their kindness and appreciation, while others express a continuous outpouring of support? Are you striving to see the best in others, or do you project your own struggles and weaknesses on to them?

We sometimes seek out friends who fill a certain void. They might be the listener we never had as a child or the leader who takes charge of our follower personality. Friendships can grow between a mentor and a mentee or between coworkers or people who are placed in the same location at the same time during a pivotal point in their lives. But these connections aren't always enough to sustain a long-term, healthy friendship. These connections, however, do allow for us to learn from each person who crosses our paths. Each interaction, friendship, and association is our opportunity to recognize goodness in another. Lasting friendships require an investment of ourselves.

As you give all of your relationships a checkup this year, don't forget to examine your friendship-ability. The things you need from others are very likely the things they need from you. This clarity will help you value the people in your life and be grateful for those who have been a part of it along the way.

Shedding Light

- Are you the friend you want others to be?

- How have you aligned yourself with people who are healthy for you/not healthy for you?

- See each relationship in your life with new eyes. Focus on the goodness that each person offers.

Prayer

I want a pure heart, God. Help me to hold back feelings of judgment or envy. Give me a desire to see the good in everyone. If there are people in my life who are hurtful, give me the strength to truly see those situations so that there can be healing.

Afterglow

I will welcome each person in my life with an embrace of acceptance and grace. And I will let go of those who are destructive so that there can be healing.

Beneath the Surface Tension

Ciúnas gan uaigneas

(GAELIC FOR "QUIETNESS WITHOUT LONELINESS")

Busyness keeps us operating in stress mode. When we awaken to an overflowing mental in-box, our thoughts shift to immediate tasks, daily goals, and hourly survival needs. We remain on the surface level of our spiritual and emotional lives. An inquiry from a friend about how we are doing might lead us to dig a bit deeper for a few moments, but quickly our personal filters shift us back to surface dialogue. While writing a reflective email, we might contemplate our more significant needs, but a new email arrives and we return to the tricky business of juggling tangents.

Lighting a candle and spending moments in silence gives you time to explore who you are apart from today's emergent needs. You can't ignore what is on your plate because that is what you do when you're living in the present. But if your present never involves excavating thoughts that go beyond immediate needs, in-the-moment grumbles, and brief-encounter small talk, you will eventually disconnect from your heart, spirit, and God's leading from within. What might appear to be a well-managed life to the world is more often a life held together purely by surface tension. One break in the constant noise, the anxious routine, and everything will spill. Learn to be still and quiet without feeling alone. God is in that stillness.

Sit in silence for a time of prayer and exploration as you sink into the ideas, feelings, and dreams you've been ignoring. Make time to breathe and to question the way things are going and to take note of what you feel. Break through that surface tension and enjoy riding the waves of possibility that will flood over you. You will be refreshed and reminded how exciting it is to live a deeper life connected to God and his leading.

Shedding Light

- Give yourself the gift of knowing your heart more intimately.

- Do you feel alone when you take a moment to be quiet? Discover the companionship and comfort of the quiet by introducing the practice of solitude and prayer into your life.

Prayer

Why do I run from silence? The peace of a still moment? I know you are there, Lord, waiting for me to express my life and to listen to your leading and whispers of grace.

Afterglow

I will introduce five minutes of quiet time into my life each day this week, and I will increase that time by one minute each following week.

Growing a Problem

*Some people are making such thorough plans
for rainy days that they aren't enjoying today's sunshine.*

WILLIAM FEATHER

With a handful of snow and a fresh trail of more white ahead, I can easily turn a wimpy cluster of water and air into a rather large, dense mass. I spent a childhood indulging in this metamorphic process of turning a small lump into a large mound. Given the right conditions, I could even grow that small lump into the impressive bulges of a life-sized snowperson. Maybe this is why I am so diligent at rolling small problems around in fresh patches of thought. Each roll adds weight and mass, giving the problem a much more substantial position in my mind. When my conditions are just right for negativity— a bad experience, an anxious heart, naysayers around me, or a rough self-image day—that hypothetical what-if? is no longer miniscule but looks life sized and rather daunting. It is so big, in fact, that it can cast a shadow on today's decisions, attitude, and perspective.

Is there a mass of what-ifs you are rolling around in your mind with vigor and determination? Isn't it amazing how it can actually *feel* productive to grow our problems? I've real-ized over the years that if I let some sunshine in, these growing blobs begin to disappear. Positive thoughts, prayer, prayers of others, encouraging readings, enjoyable activities, and friend-ships will warm up my thoughts and start to shift the internal storm toward a brighter day. The next time you roll the same old problems around a new day's worth of clean thoughts, step into the warmth of good thinking and positive actions. It is so much better to see your problems melt down and avoid a mental meltdown of your own.

Shedding Light

- How have you snowballed a possible problem into a certain obstacle?

- Why do you think you bring old problems or worries back into each day's new thoughts? Where did you learn to do this? Do you worry what would fill your mind if you let go of these old patterns?

Prayer

I'm so tired of these anxieties and hypothetical problems, God. I know I waste the provision of each day on these useless worries. Help me to let go of them and to see them for what they are… obstacles I myself have created. I want to see how my life will be filled with goodness when I let go of fear.

Afterglow

When old worries pop into my mind today, I will say "today is for the light of new thoughts" and will feel the old melt away.

Imperfect Offerings

Give all thou canst; high Heaven rejects the lore
Of nicely-calculated less or more.

WILLIAM WORDSWORTH

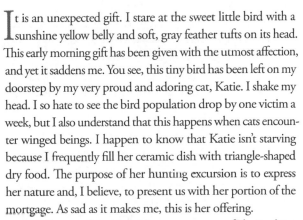

It is an unexpected gift. I stare at the sweet little bird with a sunshine yellow belly and soft, gray feather tufts on its head. This early morning gift has been given with the utmost affection, and yet it saddens me. You see, this tiny bird has been left on my doorstep by my very proud and adoring cat, Katie. I shake my head. I so hate to see the bird population drop by one victim a week, but I also understand that this happens when cats encounter winged beings. I happen to know that Katie isn't starving because I frequently fill her ceramic dish with triangle-shaped dry food. The purpose of her hunting excursion is to express her nature and, I believe, to present us with her portion of the mortgage. As sad as it makes me, this is her offering.

As I dispose of the bird, I have a moment of clarity about my offerings to God. Many times I've substituted something that would truly please God—my commitment, faithfulness, time, undivided attention—for the remains of something I pursued out of my nature—halfhearted joy, a reluctant tithe, a wimpy effort to extend compassion, etc. I don't even have the disclaimer of sincere kitty-pride as I lay my weak gifts out before God with a groan of embarrassment.

How many times have your choices saddened God? Last week, did he pick up your failed attempt to forgive with a rubber-gloved hand, shake his head, and add it to the pile of past offerings with a sigh? Pay attention to what you are pursuing with all of your heart and soul. It might be more about what interests you than about what pleases God.

Shedding Light

- Take a look at those gifts you place on God's porch week after week. Are they about you or about God?
- When do you give of yourself completely? Is it in one area of your life or during certain times of your life? Ask yourself why you hold back in other arenas or during other times.

Prayer

God, I'm sorry for the times when I lift up my stuff, my desires, my pursuits and call them offerings. I know I often give you the remains of my failed efforts rather than the whole of me. May I learn to put aside my nature so that I can adopt your nature and your heart for life and others.

Afterglow

Today I'll watch for opportunities to give out of a desire to please God rather than myself.

Light a Candle
for Gratitude

Highlights

Light tomorrow with today.

ELIZABETH BARRETT BROWNING

I had a good math teacher who had one flaw—he always used sports scenarios to explain mathematical principles. Yet here I am about to jump into a sports analogy. First, I'll preface it with this: I'd rather sit on nails than sit through a full game of televised football. However, I can tolerate watching the highlights on the weekend sports shows. Watching a 15-minute compilation of a week's worth of sports makes sense to me. Show me the good stuff. Show me who made great moves and saved the day. Point out a team's progress and then show me the scores and rankings. It's very uplifting to see clip after clip of good plays. The spiritual lesson? If we were given the opportunity to watch, every weekend, our personal highlights of the week, would we be inspired? Would there be enough material to even fill the sports show format?

When I think of highlights, I think in terms of successful passes and catches. Giving and receiving. Simple enough. Did you give words of praise to others? When a friend tried to tell you about her struggle, did you receive her words with tenderness and care? Highlights also reveal how a play was supposed to go and then how it was carried out, for better or for worse. If we diagrammed our actions for a week, would the white chalk marks look like a kindergartner's sugar-induced drawing or would they show that we were following the plan given to us by a higher authority?

I think we would all benefit from the opportunity to review our lives now and then. Play by play. Decision by decision. Move by move. We'll have fewer fumbles when we understand that we are given our position and our ability for a higher purpose…so that we can heed God's calls daily and create a life filled with highlights tomorrow. Go team!

Shedding Light

- How do you spark the light of hope for others?

- When were you last inspired by the words or actions of another? Consider how you can model them. Ask God what you have to give today and give it.

Prayer

So many fumbles, Lord! I have many regrets, but now I want to see each day as my chance to serve you, bring about light for others, and inspire the hearts of friends and strangers with simple kindnesses.

Afterglow

To follow God's plan for my day, I will watch closely for ways to make the most of the day and to build up others.

Daily Sacraments

For everything that lives is holy, life delights in life.

WILLIAM BLAKE

I went to a local restaurant and ordered a very basic meal of rice, black beans, veggies, and chicken with a dash of salsa. I gave my name with my order to the manager at the counter, and I retreated to a corner table to wait. A few minutes later, I saw the man step out from the kitchen. He called out my name and I stood up to meet him halfway. I reached for my take-out container, and as I did, the manager paused and communicated what my order was. As he carefully listed off the ingredients, they each sounded rich and satisfying. I nodded my thanks, received the cardboard container, and headed out the door to walk several blocks back home. All the while I was thinking about how his presentation of the meal felt like an offering of the sacraments. His manner and our exchange made my ordinary order feel important and personal.

My take-out meal was healthy but it wasn't remotely holy. This sacrament wasn't communion. And yet, this moment of simple generosity and attention revealed how we can transform ordinary exchanges into meaningful acts of grace. When our manner is deliberate and gentle, we meld the sacred with the everyday. We can do this for others in our lives. Saying grace before dinner will make the time shared over that meal more special. Shaking hands with a stranger as we ask their name will make our connection more personal. Asking how someone is and caring about the answer will expand our relationships.

Take time to slow down and have genuine exchanges with people. Whether you are giving or receiving, do so with a grateful heart. And when you can, be sure to list off the ingredients that blend to create your good life…make this an offering of thanks to God.

Shedding Light

- How can you bring the sacred into your daily life?

- When have you witnessed a moment that melded the sacred with the ordinary? How did it make you feel?

- What are your main obstacles to nurturing holiness and goodness? Busyness, self-importance, surface living, uncertain how to begin?

Prayer

Show me how to express my awe in your goodness and grace, God. Lead me to seek out ways to honor faith and to serve you. Give me your heart for others so that generosity and hospitality become my way of interaction.

Afterglow

I will enter my day with the word "sacred" on my mind. I will give and receive the daily sacraments of grace and belief.

Benediction of Gratitude

*We need to remind each other that the cup of sorrow
is also the cup of joy, that precisely what causes us
sadness can become the fertile ground for gladness.*

HENRI NOUWEN

"Today is the day the Lord has made; let us rejoice and be glad
in it." My husband calls this out in the morning. If I haven't
hit my snooze alarm thrice, I call out "Amen" in response. And
I mean it. Awe and pride both rise up when I hear this morning blessing because I know Marc is choosing to sip from the
cup of gratitude. And he is sharing that cup with me. Who
am I to refuse to drink? I have not faced the hardships he has
in the past few years. I have supported him, I have stood by
him, I have prayed for him, but I have not faced the physical
trial that has been his journey. The gifts of compassion, prayer,
and generosity I have known during this trial lead me to the
cup. When I witness my husband's willingness to celebrate a
day, not because it is easy but because it is a gift from God, then
I am compelled to lift the cup to my lips.

If we reject gratitude until we experience a perfect day or
our life becomes an uncomplicated bliss-fest, then we will not
partake of it. Perhaps ever. You don't produce gratitude. Success doesn't produce gratitude. Gratitude comes from God. Do
you recognize that your present reason for perseverance is also

---

Light a Candle for Gratitude

a reason to be grateful? Can you face a future of unknowns, standing on some hard-to-face knowns, and still rejoice in the possibility of hope and goodness? Will you give your heartache to God so that something meaningful can be made from your pain? If so, then you have come to the cup of gratitude. Drink. Today *is* the day the Lord has made; let us rejoice and be glad in it. Can I hear an "amen"?

Shedding Light

- What have you let keep you from sipping from the cup of gratitude?
- Find ways to open up your life to receive it. Consider focused times of prayer or journaling. Create lists of what you are thankful for this week, this season.

Prayer

I've wanted my trials to be taken from me, and yet they lead me to the cup of gratitude. I am ready to be filled and renewed.

Afterglow

I will see gratitude not as a reflection of my circumstances, but as a response to my God.

Change of Tune

Change your thoughts, and change your world.

NORMAN VINCENT PEALE

Did you get one too? That broken record…the one that sticks on negative phrases and repeats them over and over? How did so many of us end up buying into a faulty record? Maybe it ended up as a white elephant gift and we've all attended too many holiday or company parties. The great news is that mental records, just like the physical ones, can be replaced by remixed downloads.

Light a candle for this round. Now let the record play. Listen to the lists of perceived faults or mistakes. Don't forget the one about how you don't make good choices, never have, never will. And let's see what else…you can't lose weight because you're lazy. Or, you can't try something new because you're not smart enough. Dig into your broken record collection from way back. The oldies but goodies. Maybe comments from your parents or from a friend who made herself feel better by putting you down? If your home was governed by anger, do you re-create that world with your self-talk and your actions? If your family struggled financially or emotionally, do you tell yourself you're destined for the same?

This is your chance to toss out the broken pieces and download thoughts of love, blessing, and healing. Today, for every negative chorus you can list, think of something you are grateful for, something you are good at, something you have set as a goal, and something you know to be true about God's love for you—which is so great and deep that it replaces the shame and the sin, the harm and the hurt, the tears and the transgressions.

You are not going through your old broken records in order to dust them off and keep them handy in your life today. This is your chance to say goodbye. And as your connection to God becomes stronger, the list of reasons to be grateful will rise to the surface of your mind and spirit. God's promises will play, over and over, and your heart will be glad.

Shedding Light

- I know you can quote the bad stuff. It's inscribed on your heart. Let yourself throw away those records.

- Have you passed along your broken sayings and beliefs to others? Restore in them a sense of joy and gratitude by building them up and modeling for them God's grace.

Prayer

Forgive me for replacing your love and truths with the lies I tell myself. I think I even speak negative words in my sleep. God, I am grateful for your words of healing and mercy. They fill me with hope. Amen.

Afterglow

I will enjoy a morning, a day, a week of thinking differently and believing in God's love.

Drawing from the Well

Once we have only God to depend on...
then we can with joy "draw water out of
the wells of salvation" (Isaiah 12:2-3).

Catherine Marshall

Imaginary Counselor: You seem to have a lot on your mind.

You: I have to juggle a lot these days. I can't keep track, and it overwhelms me. Life is hard and complicated and...

IC: And?

You: Lonely.

IC: How is your giving these days?

You: I told you. I have a lot to juggle.

IC: Maybe you're holding on to too much.

You: What's the alternative?

IC: Give to others. Share your burdens and your blessings.

You: What would I have to offer right now?

IC: Time. Kindness. Service. A welcome smile. An offer of support. A phone call.

You: Those things you listed...I need them!

IC: Start giving from a place of gratitude.

You: I told you…life is hard. I don't know that I'm really…

IC: Grateful?

You: Yes. That sounds so awful. I used to thank God for my blessings. I don't know what happened.

IC: You tried to generate gratitude from your own reserves, from your own circumstances, and you couldn't. Gratitude comes from the well of God's heart. It never runs dry. In fact, it overflows. Are you going to be renewed in your gratitude?

You: I'm ready to draw from the well of God's love and grace. What do I do?

IC: Start giving.

Shedding Light

- Are you willing to give even when you are in a place of hardship?
- I've had to rely on God's well of grace and gratitude. I know he is faithful. Bring your pail and join me here.

Prayer

Lord, I will come to your heart, your love, and, abundance to draw what I need…not only so that I can be filled, but so that I can share with others.

Afterglow

I will act out my belief that God's love is endless and that his grace flows without limit.

Light a Candle
for Peace

Faith in Faith

He said to me, "My grace is sufficient for you,
for my power is made perfect in weakness."

2 CORINTHIANS 12:9 NIV

It can happen like this: On a Monday we are doing well and feeling secure about life and our place in the world. We pray, we believe, we lean on God. On a Wednesday we encounter a sorrow that shakes our foundation of faith. By Saturday we are trying to process our difficult circumstance and regain our balance and keep on moving in our original direction, but it isn't easy to move forward when you are reaching out to stabilize yourself with every step you take. It is deeply painful to question God's care or God's presence, but I believe these times of conflict happen to many of us. Having faith might just be the most difficult, perpetual action we could commit to.

What we need to say to those who are experiencing times of doubt and spiritual chaos—and what we personally need to hear when we are struggling—is that it is sufficient to have faith in faith for this time. When your mind is scattered and you spend sleepless nights picking apart everything you believe, from your sense of self to your sense of the Creator, it is okay to turn to and rest in the heart knowledge of faith's power. While we might not believe it during times of sadness or hardship, it is through such storms that we become more certain that

God's love is real. God doesn't stand on the other side of the chasm of belief and watch you struggle. God is willing to be in the struggle with you, even if you don't understand how grace works, even when you become cynical about the possibility of unconditional love, and especially when you wonder if you have what it takes to trust completely.

You don't have to have all the answers to the questions right now…but you do need one answer. Yes, faith in faith alone is enough for right now.

Shedding Light

- How can having faith in faith free you from your burden of uncertainty during hard times?

- Do you put too much pressure on yourself to have all of the answers…the God-answers of life? You might be trying to replace faith with knowledge and control. Return to faith.

Prayer

Resting in faith sounds so good to me. My heart has been broken, and I don't understand life right now. Why do I try to figure out everything and fix everything in my own power? I am tired and uncertain. I have moments of doubt. Give me rest today, God. For today, it is enough to have faith in faith.

Afterglow

Through prayer, I will exchange my control, doubt, and pain for the peace of faith.

Nothing Too Great

All we are asked to bear we can bear. That is a law of the spiritual life. The only hindrance to the working of this law, as of all benign laws, is fear.

ELIZABETH GOUDGE

After some years of expending significant energy, time, and effort toward one area of life, I feel weary. Have you been through a season of depletion? Did you lose hope or love? Physically, such a time is demanding. You crave heavy sleep that carries you through dream after dream, yet rest comes only in fits and starts. Spiritually, such a time is distancing. You want connection to God, yet intimacy is elusive.

These times of emptiness become experiences of healing and peace. God longs for us to be whole and complete. Our circumstances may have taken away something of great importance in our lives, but when we offer our hearts to God as empty, hurting vessels, he fills them until they can hold no more. Healing can be painful. As peace pours back into our lives, it will stretch our hearts and dreams. We have to relearn what it feels like to be replete with God's love and satiated with the sweetness of hope.

When you spend sleepless nights and difficult days measuring your emptiness, do not worry that its dimensions are too great for your human efforts to ever fill. No pain or weariness is too big to be brought to the Source of your joy and healing. God's mercy will keep on flowing until pain is replaced by peace and your loneliness is replaced by lasting communion.

Shedding Light

- Do you believe that God is greater than the hurt you feel?

- When has fear pulled you back into the emptiness?

- What do you hope for in God? Healing, rest, peace, answers, forgiveness? He offers these to you.

Prayer

Fill me with your love, God. Replace the ache of pain with the ease of peace. I've held back my hurt because I saw no way around it or through it. You are that way. Lead me into your mercy.

Afterglow

I will let go of the physical or spiritual trial that has emptied my heart and ask to be filled with hope.

Borrowed Longings

*The really important things are not houses
and lands, stocks and bonds, automobiles and
real estate, but friendships, trust, confidence,
empathy, mercy, love and faith.*

BERTRAND RUSSELL

———— ∽ ————

Our moods, priorities, and decisions can be swayed by a very important factor. I'm not talking about our diet or finances. I'm looking at a more internal force: our longings. What are you striving to accomplish or become? Do you crave attention and love? Have you always wanted a large family? Do you long for a big house with a perfect yard? Are there days you wish you were in a different marriage or a new family entirely?

Longings can draw us closer to our purpose if they are directed toward God. When our hearts long for God's love and for his grace to sweep over our lives, we are looking for healing and a chance to belong. But when our longings become a persistent grumble, one long sigh of dissatisfaction, then they are no longer tied to our dreams and our purpose but are anchored to malcontent and the world's sense of fulfillment and entitlement. In fact, I think more than a few of us are carrying a sense of regret or envy over things that aren't even our longings to begin with. We listen to the expressed dissatisfaction of our peers, coworkers, celebrities, or friends, and soon our life that seemed fine the day before is, over time, cast in a gloomy shade of gray. This is when we truly believe that life would be better, if not perfect, in that house, with that spouse, with those clothes, in that car, near that beach, in that size dress.

Notice where daydreams take your heart and be willing to go deeper. When you're frustrated about a situation or a relationship, consider whether you are measuring it up against someone else's version of the good life. Redirect your longings toward the things of God—compassion, love, patience, perseverance, kindness, and integrity. These desires will not mislead you. They will fill your life and satisfy your heart.

Shedding Light

- Whose longings are you striving to fulfill? Have you borrowed a few from parents, friends, our culture?

- Which godly longings would you like to focus on?

- Which borrowed longings are you ready to let go of?

Prayer

I realize I live my life with a twinge of discontentment because I'm pursuing things that have nothing to do with my purpose. God, give me a peace for those pursuits that are of you and your direction for me.

Afterglow

I will pursue the dreams that have my name on them…the dreams that are shaped for me by a personal God.

Open Windows

*The windows of my soul I throw
Wide open to the sun.*

JOHN GREENLEAF WHITTIER

One rainy Thursday night, I was walking along an urban residential block enjoying the darkening sky of dusk. An ambulance siren shrieked at a nearby hospital. A car alarm sounded two blocks over. And an electric streetcar heading north whirred on its tracked course behind me. These sounds all faded from my attention as I approached an old brick apartment building and heard an appealing song being played somewhere overhead. I glanced into the drizzle and saw an open window a couple of floors up. A single light was on. I could hear two girls laughing and talking above the music coming from speakers somewhere just inside the ornately trimmed sill. If I could go by their music choice, I'd bet that these girls have great taste in food, friends, and movies.

I like what open windows can offer a passerby. When we open up our souls to those who pass by and through our lives, there is a lot we can share in a matter of moments. If we project an authentic bit of who we are to each person we encounter, we will offer them a glimpse of who God is and what God is doing through us. Let's hope they sense warmth, kindness, and peace. Let's pray they hear the good music of praises and wisdom. And when sadness is raining on their lives, may the other sounds fade to the background as they hear the gentle music of our hearts welcoming them to friendship, laughter, and a warm place to be themselves.

Shedding Light

- Do you open up the windows to your soul so that others see who you are?

- Are you one to quickly invite another to an authentic conversation, sincere laughter, and genuine connection? Or do you keep a barrier between you and others until they have proven themselves in some way?

Prayer

You bring joy and peace into my life, God. In those moments when I make a connection with another person, I feel a sense of connection to you. Show me when and how I hold back my true self so that I can open up and be willing to extend a generous heart and a listening spirit to another.

Afterglow

I will watch for and welcome opportunities, people, connection, possibility, leading, and the peace of an open life and faith.

Missing Peace

God can make you everything you want to be,
but you have to put everything in His hands.

MAHALIA JACKSON

What is missing from your life? There are two extreme ways that some people think on this question: They build a life around their personal answer. Whether their void is loneliness or value or love, they focus on that one area with such determination that they sacrifice other areas. Or they build a life focused on the question itself. They don't know what is missing, but they do know they don't have peace. Their quest to answer the question becomes a singular journey that doesn't lead very far and the answer is always out of reach.

This question usually sneaks up on us when we face a transition or when we observe someone else's change in season: a new baby, a graduation, a funeral. You might try to shake it the way you would a tagalong younger sibling, but when you acknowledge what is missing you can begin to pray for that area daily.

I'm talking a lot about the question and less about the answer because we each have a different void, a different bit of longing which will vary as our life circumstances change. But if we trace the missing piece back to its root—the desire for love, the need for security, the hope of healing—we can rest in the answers we are given by our Creator. Unconditional love, the assurance of grace, the promise of wholeness.

The peace-filled life is not one large puzzle that requires precisely shaped or colored pieces; the peace-filled life is fluid, beautiful, and abundant. Have you been so focused on getting married or accomplishing a career goal or having a kitchen with green marble tiles that you haven't asked and answered the important question: "Am I ready to let go of the missing piece in order to have God's peace?"

Shedding Light

- Have you pursued one aspect of life with such fervency that you've sacrificed other areas?
- When do you allow yourself to explore those meaning-of-life thoughts? If the answer is "never," then take time to do that now.
- When do you feel most at peace? Can you allow that sense of God's peace to fill you during other times and during other circumstances?

Prayer

God, I've felt that I've been missing out on life because of one missing piece. Help me to have hope in this area and also to turn my focus toward you and all that you provide. I give you my concerns, my sense of loss, and my hopes…and I will step into your wholeness and abundance.

Afterglow

I will give all areas of my life to God. I'll do that today, tomorrow, and the next day so that it becomes the way I live out my hope.

Freed During the Resistance

*His gifts are free for the taking, but I cannot
take these gifts if my hands are already full
of my own weapons of self-protection.*

KATHERINE WALDEN

I wasn't imprisoned for writing a radical underground news-
paper. I didn't plot a rebellion on a college campus. But in
my adult life, I've been a part of a resistance. At some point I
started to resist the abundant, complete life God was presenting.
I said no thanks to travel when staying home sounded more
comfortable. I shook my head when the intimidating challenge
of trying something new arose without advance notice. I held
up my hands to ward off a life trial and then spent the entire
span of that trial resisting the lessons it was teaching.

But I can't tell you why. It's funny how you think you know
yourself really well but then discover that you've been doing
things behind your back. Life-changing things. Like saying no
to the life nudged your way over and over again. As I look back
at all these paths not taken, these refusals, these excuses that
cloud my perception even today…I'm pretty sure I've done
more resisting than embracing.

If you can look back on your life and witness a picket line
of complaints, excuses, rants, and refusals, then you might be
a part of your own resistance. I have wisdom for both of us:

You can't hug something when your arms are folded across your chest in defiance. That sounds a lot like a quip to be attributed to a spunky Southern grandmother, but whatever way you hear it, read it, or take it in is fine by me...as long as you embrace its truth and stop resisting the very lovely life being offered to you.

Shedding Light

- What do you resist the most in your life? Help, love, tenderness, challenge, sadness, growth? Take time to prayerfully figure out why you say no to good things.

- Resistance comes from a place of self-protection. See if you can view each decision and opportunity as a way to peace. Welcome these issues into your life so that you can see how God's peace surpasses our very limited understanding of what is good for us and what can harm us.

Prayer

Just this week I said no to something I was supposed to say yes to without fear and without resistance. God, grant me the seed of hope I need to unfold my arms and to unfold a life of wonder.

Afterglow

I will say yes to more things this week. And I'll accept the good, the bad, the doubts, and the duty tied to each opportunity.

Light a Candle
for Faith

What Are You Looking For?

People see God every day. They just don't recognize him.

PEARL BAILEY

———⚬———

When Jesus came on the scene, he did not meet the list of requirements people had for the Messiah. He spoke as a king might...about the kingdom of God...but he directed his attention to the poor, the diseased, the outcasts. He was smart and wise and well versed in the Jewish law, but he challenged those leaders who represented the law. He spoke with authority and power, yet he showed great humility and mercy. He could command an audience of thousands with his message but he frequently tended to the broken and the lonely one-on-one. Jesus communicated a simple message, of serving God and loving one another, and yet he was a complicated version of who the Messiah was. Jesus shook up established thoughts about religion and faith. He made the message and commitment personal and the call to learn and serve universal.

I'm not surprised people were torn between their religious affiliations and traditions and the appealing, radically different approach of Jesus. Aren't we just as torn today? We might be Christians for many years when suddenly we realize we are so immersed in the world of religion and tradition that we've forgotten how radical the love of Christ is. We feel, with a renewed heart, touched by the call to intimate relationship Jesus places on our hearts.

Do you still expect Jesus to look a certain way? Do you wait for him to act in a commanding, kingly manner rather than through gentle leading and grace? He is powerful and merciful. And he will meet you where you are. He will point out that which is solely religion and that which is wholly faith. He will see your brokenness and talk to you one-on-one. And he will say "follow me." Don't look any further.

Shedding Light

- Do you keep looking for a different version of Jesus? Are you watching for a God who fits your job description for a messiah or are you looking for the real thing? The one who knows your heart and who loves the unlovable?

- Jesus wants to speak to each of us one-on-one. Have you been willing to listen?

Prayer

God, I will set aside my expectations and my demands and my limited perspective of you. Forgive me for accepting only a part of you. Lead me to deeper relationship with the real you. Show me what it is to follow you and to live in the power of grace.

Afterglow

I will stop limiting God with my human perspective so that I can become a seeker of truth and transformation.

Walking Upright

*Trust in the Lord with all your heart
and lean not on your own understanding;
in all your ways acknowledge him,
and he will make your paths straight.*

PROVERBS 3:5-6 NIV

⸺⸺❧⸺⸺

L ike a lot of women, I slouch my shoulders. When I take inventory of my walk after I get up in the morning, inevitably I find that my shoulders slump inward and I lean forward rather than walk upright. No wonder I am tired much of the day…I start out walking like a woman who carries all her belongings on her back. With concerted effort I'm trying to correct that as I walk around the house or out in the world. Chin down, shoulders back and relaxed, hips aligned with spine, core tightened. It's a lot to keep track of, but I feel better and stronger when I'm walking upright and as tall as a short person is able.

Our walks of faith need similar assessment from time to time. We fall into patterns of movement and adopt habits that compromise our spiritual strength, the integrity of our position about life and love, and our direction. We slouch, we stumble, we lean forward with our own objectives rather than resting back in God's purposes for us. Our decisions, even our intentional spiritual decisions, are made from an off-balance perspective. We end up living lives not aligned with God and his strength.

No wonder we become so tired. No wonder our physical and emotional positioning makes us look like women who carry all of their burdens their shoulders and their minds.

It is a good day to walk forward, free of those heavy burdens. Did you really want them to begin with? Sharing your load with your Creator is not shirking responsibility; it is your first step toward aligning your steps, choices, decisions, and dreams with his purpose for you.

Shedding Light

- How have your steps detoured from what you believe to be right or true?

- What has been your position while walking in faith? Do you stand strong and walk as one who knows the gifts of grace and purpose?

- As you rest in God, which burden will you lift up to him first?

Prayer

I've noticed how crooked my path has been these past few years. From where I stand, I can barely see the horizon of your purpose, God. Redirect my steps, my posture of faith, my quest for value. I want to know that I'm walking forward with the strength of someone loved, supported, and known by you.

Afterglow

I will focus on how I stand in my faith. As I release each burden to God's care, I'll physically, emotionally, and spiritually feel the difference in my life.

How to Rebuild a Life

*Our real blessings often appear to us
in the shape of pains, losses, and disappointments.*

Joseph Addison

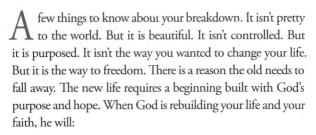

A few things to know about your breakdown. It isn't pretty to the world. But it is beautiful. It isn't controlled. But it is purposed. It isn't the way you wanted to change your life. But it is the way to freedom. There is a reason the old needs to fall away. The new life requires a beginning built with God's purpose and hope. When God is rebuilding your life and your faith, he will:

- Break down the walls built during past pain to build up the power of forgiveness.

- Break down the coldness of religiosity to build up the intimacy of personal faith.

- Break down the stereotype of success to build up the truth of abundant living.

- Break down the need for control to build up your readiness for divine guidance.

- Break down the expectations you've built up to build up your hope for the promises of God.

Our transformation is taking place when we watch life as we've known it crumble around the edges and sink into the faulty foundation of anger, pain, regret, and emptiness. It might look like loss, but it is the image of gaining abundance. It might feel like starting over, but it is really about moving forward. Faith wasn't built in a day. Okay, I borrowed part of that line from something else, but it's still true. Things that last aren't built overnight. We can receive salvation in an instant, but faith is ongoing and evolving because it is a relationship with a living God. Those times of tearing down will lead to the rebuilding and restoration of your faith and your life. Don't try to salvage the ruins. Spend time with *the* Architect and celebrate the new plans that are unfolding.

Shedding Light

- The word "blessing" is thrown around a lot. What does it mean to you?
- Can you view a recent loss or struggle as a blessing? Do you see how your deconstruction is leading to the rebuilding of faith and hope?
- The new thing God is creating in your life will lead you forward. Trust in that.

Prayer

God, as much as I want to rest in the blessings of this trial, I'm not there yet. Today, can I just rest in your shelter? I look forward to the restoration I know will come. Your faithfulness in the past builds up my faith today, and I am grateful.

Afterglow

I will stop building walls so that I can see the life being rebuilt by God's compassion and peace.

It's Personal

*All I have seen teaches me
to trust the Creator for all I have not seen.*

RALPH WALDO EMERSON

❧

H ow did you come to faith? What was it that beckoned
you to belief? During my years of interacting with others
who profess similar beliefs, I've noticed that we each have our
own personal understanding and tenderness toward our faith.
Often it is directly related to whichever wonder, truth, or gift
that revealed God's presence to us in the first place.

So what led you to that moment of faith? What caught your
attention in the middle of a hardship or a season of busyness?
What made your heart stir with that sense of home and belonging that God's presence provides? Was it the:

- Perspective of the eternal in light of life's frailty
- Gift of salvation
- Surprise and comfort of God's love
- Unexpected mercy
- Intimacy with and accessibility to God
- Wisdom of the Bible
- Manifestations of faith in someone else's life
- Transforming power of grace
- Tenderness and profundity of Jesus
- Miracle of resurrection

Was your invitation to faith through an encounter with Christ when you were actively searching—or when you were going about your own business and not giving the Creator much thought? God is full of surprises. Maybe it took a time of extreme loneliness or dissatisfaction before you recognized that God's art is wholeness. It is good to recognize how we have come to this place of faith. Be grateful for your journey. Be thankful for the faith journeys of others. You and I…we are blessed with distinct gifts and purpose; it shouldn't be a surprise that he calls us to his heart in very unique, personal ways. That's how God works. You've heard…in mysterious ways.

Shedding Light

- How were you called to faith? Is it hard for you to relate to people who came to faith for different reasons?

- Are you still observing rather than residing in belief? What fears or reservations do you have?

- Try to see God's art of wholeness in others. We all bear the Creator's signature.

Prayer

God, I'm so grateful for this journey. I've been through many things since I first believed in you and felt that sense of home and belonging. Thank you for your faithfulness, even during my times of uncertainty.

Afterglow

I'll reflect on how I came to faith, and I'll celebrate all that this path of belief offers me personally.

Believing in Others

There are different kinds of gifts, but the same Spirit.
There are different kinds of service, but the same Lord.
There are different kinds of working, but the
same God works all of them in all men.

1 CORINTHIANS 12:4-6 NIV

———※———

Reliance on God is an important part of faith. Reliance on how God works in the hearts and lives of others is equally important. I'm always amazed by the goodness and selflessness that people demonstrate. They donate time and money to local charity organizations, contribute to vital causes across the globe, stand up for the rights of people they will never meet, pray for and serve the needs of acquaintances and strangers, and respond to God's leading.

All of God's children are made in his image. Some might not know him intimately yet or believe that he can move through them toward a personal purpose, but God still leads, changes hearts, convicts the spirit, inspires transformation.

Our dependence on God should not put us at risk of becoming completely independent of others. Have you ever needed support desperately but wouldn't trust others to step up, so you didn't even ask? Or have you requested help and expected nobody to follow through…and been pleasantly surprised? Have faith in others. Watch for their goodness and their good works. Every day there will be instances that remind you of the faithfulness of the heart formed by God and for God. Don't underestimate the courage and compassion of the person next door, the man looking for work, the woman at the checkout counter.

Presume the best about people, and you will discover the very best of humanity. If we commit to this perspective, we will discover the greater thing indeed…why and how "God so loved the world."

Shedding Light

- When have you been surprised by an individual's response to a need or to a community's outpouring of kindness?

- How do you respond to needs you see around you? Are you depending on God to have other people step up while you hold back out of fear or lack of motivation?

- Allow yourself to be amazed by compassion. Ask for help. Believe in the faithfulness of others.

Prayer

I am not always quick to believe in others. I want them to prove themselves. Guide my heart away from fear so that I can open my eyes to the faithfulness of others. I want to see you in the goodness that is around me in friends and strangers.

Afterglow

I'll believe in the people I encounter today. I will look for and see the beauty of their potential and their heart.

Life with a View

*Life without faith in something is
too narrow a space to live.*

GEORGE LANCASTER SPALDING

After much prayer, a middle-aged woman decided to take a long-delayed trip to a foreign city. She arrived at her hotel filled with excitement. She told the manager that this trip was answered prayer. His face turned red. "We've misplaced your reservation. Please have a seat while I fix this. I'm so sorry."

"I'm not worried. Whatever room you have is fine. But…a view would be so special."

Ten minutes later the manager asked the woman to follow him. They took the elevator to the nineteenth floor. "I think you'll like this view," he said with a broad smile. The woman entered what was clearly the penthouse suite. The manager pointed out the amenities to her, but her eyes were fixed on the glass double doors which framed a breathtaking view of the city square and an exquisite park.

Every morning, the woman sipped coffee on the terrace and planned her outings. She spent evenings full of gratitude looking at the glow of lampposts in the park. On her last evening, she ordered room service so she could savor her beloved view.

The manager himself delivered the meal and asked if she would like him to start a fire in the fireplace. She pulled her glance away from the window and looked at him. "What fire-place?" she asked. He furrowed his brow, took three steps back, and opened up a set of double doors, revealing a large living area of velvet furniture and a marble mantel fireplace.

"Oh, my! I thought those doors led to another closet!"

The manager, clearly appalled, stammered for several seconds and then said, "It's so terrible! Here you are in the penthouse, on your dream trip, and you didn't get to enjoy the riches of it."

The woman laughed, turned back to the window, and sighed. "Oh, yes I did."

Shedding Light

- Are you savoring the riches of your life?

- When one of your dreams is realized, are you quick to see how it is flawed or not quite the way you imagined? Or do you focus on the beauty of the moment and the riches of a new life experience?

- Do you cherish the gifts God provides? Big, small, ordinary, miraculous?

Prayer

What have I been doing all this time? Some dreams I have put off, others I have ruined by picking them apart when they don't fit my vision of perfection. God, help me to embrace this life of mine…I don't want to miss a moment.

Afterglow

I will live richly and abundantly by savoring the view of my life.

Light a Candle
for Healing

Beauty of Resurrection

*Often, in the midst of great problems, we
stop short of the real blessing God has for us,
which is a fresh vision of who He is.*

ANNE GRAHAM LOTZ

There was a time when things changed for you and me. When losses left gaps in our dreams and swayed our paths with such force that we never quite got back on track. Many of us have spent a lifetime trying to retrieve what went missing so long ago. Whatever we have lost through mistakes, brokenness, pain, illness, or rejection leaves us with a picture of "what could have been" had those sufferings never occurred. Retrieval involves a constant desire to re-create what we had just before things shifted. Just before we lost our way. Just before we reluctantly changed our plans and dreams.

Don't confuse the human instinct of retrieval with the divine intention of resurrection. Retrieval works double-time to re-establish what was. It is a painstaking, detailed effort to put everything back in its place just so. But resurrection is God's life-giving force. It doesn't strive to repeat life because that would take away from the power that loss can bring when we understand its nature. Resurrection seeks to find what *will* be—what *can* be—because of a void, a hunger, a sorrow. It doesn't try to piece together a shabby version of an old life because it is designed to nurture, create, and establish something new. It uses the materials found in the aftermath of loss, but it never tries to return to life before that loss. There isn't power in those remnants you hold in your hand so tightly. Grab onto the life that is being created in you now. You have a new vision of life and a truer understanding of God's love and care. Beautiful and meaningful things can come of loss if we don't try to re-create something old, but prepare ourselves to embrace a new life.

Shedding Light

- Have you invested more belief in retrieval than in resurrection?
- Do you want something that replicates the past or something that transcends what is known and offers rebirth? How can you move toward the latter?
- The life lived in the power of Christ's resurrection doesn't mourn the small deaths of circumstances and seasons. This is a life that sees beginnings and restoration with each change.

Prayer

I really want to live in the power of the resurrection, Lord. I believe in transformation and a life renewed and changed by your grace. When I try to control that power by seeking to retrieve something lost, I will let go so that I can experience what can unfold through your grace.

Afterglow

I'll release my hold on those remnants of past dreams or broken paths and will reach out for the beauty of a new vision, a new truth.

Today Is for Living

Trust the past to God's mercy, the present to God's love, and the future to God's providence.

AUGUSTINE

If I were to ask you to describe your past failings and regrets, would your response be so vivid, detailed, and clear that the truth would be known—these regrets are not at all in your past but are very much in your present? Do you keep such things alive by giving them time and meditation, both of which are gifts you could be giving to God?

It's time to discard past mistakes and let yesterday do the job it was made for. Yesterday is our wise teacher when we glean its many lessons. Yesterday is our testimony when we can share about our transformation through faith and God's love. Yesterday is our reminder that God can lead us through loss and error and pride and pain. But yesterday is not our substitution for today.

If your regrets are alive and kicking, it's because you are fueling them with current thoughts and nurturing them with the oxygen and space of your present. Do you need help carrying those regrets to the foot of the cross? Are you ready to leave them for dead—because the power of the resurrection does not exist so that you can resurrect your mistakes and tend to them; it exists so that you can live abundantly in the present and have hope for a future. God's mercy has covered those difficulties and mistakes so that you can be alive in the moment and be used for greater purposes than being a life-support machine for your past. You decide each and every morning what you are going to give your presence and passions over to…the unchangeable past or the abundant and transforming present.

Shedding Light

- Which regrets do you nurture and keep alive? Are you prepared to give those up for something better?

- Old wounds can reopen time after time. I think we can become addicted to the pain and the drama. Let them truly heal so that they are a source of wisdom only.

Prayer

I'm so glad to have moved on in my life. I don't want my past failings to become my focus today. There is so much more to experience in this moment and in the future because of you. Redirect my thoughts and my sense of direction…lead me away from yesterday. It has done its job.

Afterglow

I will make sure my regrets are not being nourished by my actions and thoughts today. I'll only give energy and effort to today's hope.

Where Does It Hurt?

Let God's promises shine on your problems.

CORRIE TEN BOOM

We've come through a lot. We've faced hardships and surprises and times of need. When we've gone through an extreme difficulty and our lives seem fragmented by the cuts of sorrow, healing comes to us in different ways. Our ideas of what healing will look like and what it will free us to do once our damaged area has been repaired are so limited that we are likely to miss out on the restoration we receive.

Our healing might be taking place in a different area than the one so blatantly marked by our pain. If you've prayed for restoration in a relationship, your healing might come in the form of a new perspective about that relationship. You might need to labor through the healing and then be willing to see things anew on the other side of it. "Fix me" or "fix this" might be our heart's cry, but "one remedy suits all" is not usually how God's healing manifests in our circumstances. God is very personal in his interaction with us and how he soothes, comforts, and leads his children. Our pleas represent where we are emotionally, and often at our crisis point. And his promises are true and far reaching in our lives.

God sees our lives from beginning to end. From joy to sorrow to joy again. From need to abundance. His balm reaches the places within us we might not know are broken. So, our desire for physical healing might be met with physical healing, but be prepared to recognize the healing of an emotional wound that has long needed the balm of God's peace.

Shedding Light

- Where do you hurt? Ask God to shine light on the source of those hurts.

- Have you given thanks for past times of healing? It is important to acknowledge God's continuous work in your life. It helps you to recognize his healing in all circumstances.

Prayer

Comfort me, God. I want to have my pain soothed and my hurts healed. Prepare my heart to see and accept the way that healing is manifested in my life. Thank you for the balm of your peace and love.

Afterglow

I will share the joy of my healing with others. I will make known the goodness of redemption.

Healing After the Healing

*Birds sing after a storm; why shouldn't people feel
as free to delight in whatever remains to them?*

Rose Fitzgerald Kennedy

I've had the opportunity to lift up prayers for healing on behalf of someone I love. And together we've witnessed and experienced healing. We approach God with hearts full of gratitude for the gifts of well-being, hope, and recovery. But life doesn't look the way we thought it would. So how do we carry the hope of healing into this new experience?

Just as we don't always recognize the way healing has manifested in our bodies, relationships, hearts, and beliefs, we don't always recognize the post-healing life as the one we are intended to live out with conviction and peace. Because we are looking for a return to the life we once had, we often don't recognize the revised version of life we are given instead. Healing does not drag us back to time before the hardship; it moves us forward in knowledge, peace, and intimacy with God. This season may come with limitations and difficulties. Pressing on in this new version of life is still part of your healing. As tough as it can be, it is nevertheless a gift to see your life with new eyes, to walk with strength and appreciation toward different goals, to modify your expectations and begin living abundantly in your purpose rather than in your preconceived notions.

Loss and suffering and times of paralyzing disbelief change us from within. We do not come out the other side as the same person who went in to the trial. You are now living as a person who has been touched by transformation, renewal, and grace. Embrace the newness of healing.

Shedding Light

- Are you on the other side of a trial and still trying to make sense of how your life is now? How is it different? How is it the same?

- Can you let go of how you thought life would be after healing? God knows your life's big picture while you only experience a peephole version of it. Step forward into this healing.

- Does disbelief creep into your thoughts and prayers? Allow grace to cover your doubt.

Prayer

I'm trusting your healing, God. I welcome it and will walk forward in it. Remove those expectations I've placed on what life will be or should be. Open my heart to the wonder of your hope for me personally.

Afterglow

I won't watch for the human version of perfection, but will seek the healing that comes from the Perfector of my faith.

Gold for Sorrow

Be truly glad. There is wonderful joy ahead, even though you have to endure many trials for a little while. These trials will show that your faith is genuine. It is being tested as fire tests and purifies gold—though your faith is far more precious than mere gold.

1 PETER 1:6-7

Someone once told me that in cases of extreme grief, a gold compound has been given to patients as part of homeopathic treatment. I found that fascinating. I realize the doctor didn't say "swallow two class rings and call me in the morning." Nevertheless, I still found the concept of a precious metal used as medicine to be fascinating and poetically appropriate. Like gold, our lives can be put through the fires. The flames that touch and refine our faith are those of suffering and grief.

During our most personal and overwhelming trials, we have the gift of faith. We can lean into our faith and find rest. We can step under the covering of our faith in God for refuge. As the verse above illuminates, our faith is more precious than gold…especially for our healing. Our hope in God's peace and purpose carries us during seasons of sorrow.

When someone you care about is facing the shock of grief, it is through faith that you can be a source of strength and comfort. You can be a companion for their journey by being prayerful, tender, and generous. Your presence might encourage them to enter God's presence, where they'll experience mercy far surpassing human compassion.

As sojourners of faith, we have something else that leads us to hope and healing: "The laws of the Lord are true; each one is fair. They are more desirable than gold, even the finest gold" (Psalm 19:9-10 NLT). Try as we might, we cannot fully comprehend the mysteries of life and death, but we can cherish the pursuit of God's truth. We can desire, even in our sorrow, the beauty of a wound healed and the sacredness of a faith refined.

Shedding Light

- How has your faith been refined through the fire of trials or disappointments?

- Exchange your sorrow for God's healing. You'll get a great return on it!

- Would others in your life know the value of God's mercy? Be compassionate so that they feel the hope of healing.

Prayer

God, your comfort sustains me. You hold me up when I want to sink into grief. The refuge you provide is one that is hard for me to explain to others, and yet I hold onto it with absolute faith. You are with me in joy and in sorrow. There is nothing of greater value than your love.

Afterglow

God's truth will be my measure of what is priceless and beautiful in this season and in the future.

First Thoughts

Suffering is more or less inevitable in life, but it's not redemptive unless we allow God to make good use of it.

MOLLY WOLF

I waited for word about my husband after his surgery. It seemed forever before I could see him. By the time I did, he had surfaced from the cloud of anesthesia. He was groggy but very aware. I held his hand, kissed him, and asked him how he felt. Instead of talking about his physical state, he asked if we could pray for a guy a few curtained areas over. We couldn't see the man, but we could hear him cry out. While the staff in the overflow ICU area did all they could to ease this man's pain, we prayed for his healing and recovery.

This wasn't the first time my husband's waking thoughts were about someone else. On another occasion he prayed for a young man who had caused quite a ruckus because he wanted a cigarette before his surgery. While these loud and illogical demands had been a bit entertaining initially, we both knew that the boy was scared to undergo a serious operation. I love that my husband's initial impulse after going through his own ordeal was to seek the comfort of prayer for someone else. My husband isn't a saint, but he is kind and sensitive. His pain has led him to be more prayerful and perceptive regarding the needs of others.

When we face hardships of any kind, we might be tempted to shut down our hope and shut off those first thoughts of God's mercy. But our personal healing is possible when we are able to recognize and care about the pain of others. No matter what burdens we are dealing with, let our first thoughts each morning be of those we can lift up to God. Let's experience the healing of compassion.

Shedding Light

- Who needs thoughts and prayers of compassion? Your neighbor, a parent, a friend?

- If you are so busy that you rarely lift up your own concerns, what will it take to become quiet and still enough to pray for others?

- How have your past struggles made you more sensitive to those around you?

Prayer

God, give me a genuine heart for the needs of others. Direct my first thoughts after waking or after my trials to be of compassion. I love the idea of turning my times of pain into a greater inclination toward peace. May I draw on my own healing journey for strength and sensitivity.

Afterglow

Before I pray for myself, I will pray for others.

Light a
Candle for Joy

Inviting Joy

*Don't think so much about who is for or
against you, rather give all your care, that
God be with you in everything you do.*

THOMAS Á KEMPIS

Build a life with what you have and joy will follow. Our
worries tend to center on what won't happen, so much so
that we miss out on celebrating what will and does happen. A
friend was planning a lovely family gathering. Days in advance,
she made preparations for those who would be coming, but
her thoughts turned to those who might not show up and why.
She knew their presence would be missed and so she continued
to dwell on them. Soon she was no longer enjoying the process
of preparation; her heart had changed focus. Then her husband
pointed out a great perspective: When the day comes for the
gathering, the ones who show up are the ones to take care of.

How easy it can be to be surrounded by people we care
about and still not emotionally be with them because we are
preoccupied with the scenario that will not be, at least not this
time. If people stopped offering up themselves and their passions until they had the ultimate turnout or the perfect group,
then the careers of most musicians would end after one hotel
lounge performance. Grassroots organizations would dry up
before the mission statement could be read to those who would

benefit from its intention. And most ministries would fizzle out after one poorly attended Wednesday night meeting.

If we consider that each gathering is an opportunity of community and connection, then there isn't any good reason to fret over who isn't there. Celebrate and tend to those God brings to you and those God encourages you to join with. At your next gathering, meeting, event, or stuck-elevator incident, look around at the people you are meant to interact with and get to know. Joy is among them.

Shedding Light

- Do you focus more on what might not happen than you do on following through with your role?

- Have you pulled back from your purpose because it wasn't unfolding the way you wanted it to?

- Serve those who do show up in your life. Friends and strangers alike…they are there for a reason, and you're called to show up as well.

Prayer

Give me a heart for what does happen and for each person I meet, Lord. When I want to change plans just because things aren't turning out the way I had planned, give me a new vision and passion for what is unfolding. I will invite faith and joy to be a part of every circumstance and opportunity.

Afterglow

I will be there for others, I will invite joy, and I will be grateful for all who show up in my life.

Sabbath for Breakfast

*What I do today is important because I am
exchanging a day of my life for it.*

HUGH MULLIGAN

My quest for a good breakfast turned into a morning of simple joys. I zipped up my lightweight vest and tied a scarf around my neck as I stepped out into the cool morning. I leapt over curbside puddles and continued at a quick clip, eager for hash browns and eggs and a big coffee. Strange weather patterns this season left unlikely impressions everywhere. Yellow and purple-red fall leaves were encased in the thin layer of midwinter ice on sidewalks. I was about to lean down and salvage one when I became distracted by the woman ahead of me who juggled a briefcase and a coffee. Actually it was her pants' very wet hem that caught my attention and made me mindful of the fate of my own jeans. When a kind motorist stopped to let me cross the street, I gathered fabric at my knee to hike up my pant leg and sauntered to the other side. I felt like a Victorian woman gathering the folds of her silk skirt to make her way past a carriage.

My first restaurant choice, so nonestablishment that it's established as a town favorite, was packed. I kept walking. The second breakfast place, casual and filled with neighborhood regulars, was also overflowing. An older couple read the morning paper outside the café door. It would be a while. My feet kept moving, and I ended up at a park several blocks past my usual routes. Moms pushed strollers, young couples held gloved hands, squirrels made fast tracks through the lawn. With a quick stop at a corner establishment, I had a large coffee in my hands and kept on walking...taking in the morning. My cheeks stung from the cold and my body was invigorated from the walk.

So what if I didn't get the breakfast I was craving. It was all worth it. I highly recommend letting go of your agenda and getting lost in a morning of delicious pleasures.

Shedding Light

- Create your own Sabbath morning or day. Give rest, joy, and delight a place in your life.

- Set aside a time each day to reflect on what brings pleasure and meaning to your existence. Find ways to nurture those activities.

- Notice your life and all of its treasures. There are many. Each day is remarkable!

Prayer

Why do I let week after week go by without spending time honoring life? I live it, but I don't celebrate it. Today is a gift. Thank you, Lord, for the smallest of treasures that I uncover. Show me how to feel my life deeply.

Afterglow

I will head out today with one main goal: to breathe joy into my life and to delight in God's gifts.

Joy Harvest

*It is within my power either to serve God or not
to serve him. Serving him, I add to my own good
and the good of the whole world. Not serving him,
I forfeit my own good and deprive the world of
that good, which was in my power to create.*

Leo Tolstoy

———※———

You can tell much about a life by what it produces, by what comes forth into the world from that life's effort and existence. The work of our hands and hearts are often compared to harvests in the Bible. I consider the produce of our lives to be a matter of faith and faith alone. What pours forth from our efforts, love, and decisions reflects what is going on in our hearts. When we produce crops of complaints, arguments, destructive language and actions, self-hatred, and anger, our hearts are distant from God's leading and we've stopped tapping into God's unconditional love as our source for life.

Athenagoras, a philosopher and Christian apologist in the latter part of the second century, described the Holy Spirit as an effluence of God. That struck me as a very lovely and profound explanation. The Holy Spirit flows out of God. It makes sense to me that the outpouring of God is the Spirit. They are one, and they are separate. Ah, the confounding mystery of the Trinity. But we're not going there; we're going to your heart. If

God is your center, goodness and joy should be the effluence of your soul, your speech, your thoughts, and your intentions. Does love and abundance flow from your faith? What else does your faith produce? Is there gladness, passion for dreams, deep empathy for those in pain, a hunger for justice, and an abiding love for God and God's children?

During your time of reflection, consider what is flowing from your life. Do you emanate a peace that is of God? Instead of trying to have influence with power, money, or emotional leverage, wouldn't we offer the world much more healing and joy if we desire to be an effluence of faith?

Shedding Light

- What flows from your life now? What would you like to be the effluence of your daily living?

- The joy of a harvest is that there is abundance to share. Give of whatever God produces in your life.

- Seek the leading of the Holy Spirit so that your actions today are of God.

Prayer

Show me how to love with your love, God. Show me how to be joyful and generous with the bounty of faith you give to me daily. May I never hold back a portion of your goodness so that others receive these offerings freely.

Afterglow

I will be mindful and prayerful today so that the harvest of my efforts and actions are goodness, joy, peace, and kindness.

One, Two, Cha Cha Cha

Life is either a daring adventure or nothing.
HELEN KELLER

Maneuvering life is hard. Learning to take the right steps and make the correct moves can trip us up at any point. Even when I thought I had memorized good instruction, I've jammed my big toe, and I've leapt when I should have bowed. I have always been a closet learner, wanting to master something on my own, away from possible evaluation and scrutiny. Do you prefer to carefully orchestrate how you learn, when you learn, and when you feel ready enough to try something under the gaze of another? The shocking and embarrassing truth is that most of the time nobody is watching. But if we focus on ourselves long enough, we don't notice that no one is noticing. It isn't that people don't care; they just happen to have better things to do. Or maybe they are focused on themselves and not the woman trying to knit in public for the first time or the person working up the courage to dine alone at the corner bistro.

We command joy out of our lives when we place ourselves in charge of the learning curve. When we say no to opportunities that take us by surprise, we miss out on God's leading. You aren't the designer of your life. You make choices, and you can refuse to open up to possible failure and public ridicule, but you have to release control to God. When you or I limit the number of times we're willing to try, we're also placing a limit on how often we'll trust God. Where's the joy in that life?

We should learn something together. Let's take up something daring like juggling fire, kayaking level-5 rapids, or maybe something as radical as doing a basic, unpracticed dance move in public. That first demonstration of faith and freedom could lead us to some amazing next steps.

Shedding Light

- What have you been putting off for years because you haven't wanted to risk failure?

- Build up the courage of a friend today by encouraging their dreams and opportunities.

- Risk your heart a little, risk your pride a lot…move forward in ways that serve your spirit of joy and also in ways that serve others somehow.

Prayer

God, I claim to have faith, and yet I hold back from walking in that faith. Where is my trust in your support and your leading? Give me courage. Help me break through my hesitation, excuses, and pride to see the joy in taking leaps of faith and delighting in a life without limits.

Afterglow

I'm stepping out today and trying something new with courage and faith, focused on the joy of the activity and not on my predicted outcome.

Light Therapy

*For light I go directly to the Source of
light, not to any of the reflections.*

PEACE PILGRIM

When you are light deprived, your body hungers for light. I live in a region that has some very pleasant months but also has a very long rainy season. It's easy for moods to follow the way of weather patterns, so my husband and I bought a special blue light that is supposed to emulate sunshine and produce similar good effects in the body and mind. All that is required? You sit with the gentle blue rays beaming in your direction for 15 to 30 minutes each morning. What a worthwhile trade-off for an improved mood and better sleep.

Our spirits need light too. We crave the warmth of God's light. It offers nourishment and comfort. It fills us with hope and energy to press on. Imagine how much better our lives will be when we make a commitment to spend 15 minutes a day basking in God's light. It will improve our demeanor, outlook, attitude, perspective, motives, heart, and our sense of joy.

Do you take time to let the light in? Are you in actual spiritual darkness, spending your days under the cloud of depression, sadness, loneliness? I believe many of us and many of the people in our lives are experiencing the negative side effects of insufficient illumination. We need the radiance of promises, hope, and love. How do we seek the Source? Explore Scripture verses that speak to your needs right now. Light your candle and close your eyes and pray. Not sure what to say? Ask for joy. Ask to become a reflection of God's brilliance. Discover how to radiate the love that is given to you from God every day (well beyond a 15-minute session).

No need to flip a switch. Just turn over a new leaf, perhaps. Today is the day you can seek God's light and experience the lasting joy of everlasting love.

Shedding Light

- Have you lost the luster of a vibrant faith? Have you become dull in mind and spirit? When your thoughts are self-focused and every day is the same because you distance yourself from the spark of inspiration, you are ready for light therapy.

- For best results, place God's light at heart level. Studying about God is good, but to embrace the joy of Christ you need to direct the light of God's love at your heart. Be filled by the promises of transformation and grace. From your heart, God will illuminate the way of his will and his hope for you.

Prayer

How have I lived in such darkness for so long, God? I want the light back in my life.

Afterglow

I'll go to the light of God today to refuel, restore, and renew my sense of joy.

Ha-Ha Moment

When unhappy, one doubts everything;
when happy, one doubts nothing.

JOSEPH ROUX

Where does your happiness come from? Do you have any? Is it a quality you lack and wish you had? I've always been a bit envious of people who are quick to laugh and who find something funny at every turn. I've never been one of those people. I enjoy great humor and people who can make me laugh, but I don't start conversations with "have you heard the one about…" and I never will.

What about you? Do the demands of adulthood leave you serious and uptight? When you look toward the future, are you tense with the stress of what might happen? Happiness is a funny thing (how appropriate). It might exist in the future, but it can only be felt and experienced in the here and now. Worry seems to have a devastatingly long shelf life. That's why it's so easy to stockpile it. But happiness needs nurturing, refreshment, and the source of lasting joy—God.

Happiness and joy are not one and the same. Joy is the gift that allows you to see the silver lining of a difficult circumstance. Joy lifts you up even as responsibility and pressure might weigh you down. Joy is the catalyst for happiness. Some people operate in happy mode, but when struggles come, they don't have a foundation of joy to tap into. They need something to spark that ha-ha moment. Do you know people who are jokesters? Ha-ha moments that boost our spirits and offer us a burst of delight are fabulous (bring them on), but they *will* come and go, and our emotions can take the roller-coaster ride right along with them. But the joy of the Lord is continuous, lasting, consistent, ever-present, and, without a doubt, good for the soul.

Shedding Light

- Are you a bowl of laughs until the party is over? Keep the happiness flowing by tapping into the joy of God's love and creativity.

- When have you relied on God during a trial? Were there surprising moments of joy during a time of sorrow? Joy and sorrow can coexist when we turn to God's goodness and mercy during a season of perseverance or a moment of pain.

Prayer

I'm looking for a little levity, Lord. Help me to see the way through my trials with a heart that bursts with your love. You turn my weariness into awareness so that I can see the joy of a new day, the beauty of another person's gifts, the hope of a future, and the promise of wholeness. I am grateful.

Afterglow

I will light my candle and think of ways to build up my foundation of joy. I will rest in God's faithfulness, and I will see ha-ha moments as a gift and lasting joy as the fruit of my spiritual life.

Light a Candle
for Kindness

Mercy, Mercy Me

The wisdom that is from above is first pure,
then peaceable, gentle, willing to yield, full of
mercy and good fruits, without partiality and
without hypocrisy. Now the fruit of righteousness
is sown in peace by those who make peace.

JAMES 3:17-18 NKJV

———————⌇⌇———————

For such a gentle word, mercy is a courageous and transforming act when it is bestowed and experienced. True mercy is given by one who has power over the one who needs forgiveness. A judge grants mercy to an offender of the law. God is merciful toward his broken children. In daily life we have opportunities to offer mercy to others, and such an opportunity often involves allowing a "gotcha" moment to pass on by. Mercy very well might require that you swallow your own pride.

Rather than lord our power or influence over a friend or loved one, we can express compassion. If you're struggling to remember a time when you felt that you had any power at all, you might be looking for the wrong kind of power. We do have strength. We are placed in situations when we can and should forgive another. If a visiting child breaks a family heirloom, you have an opportunity for mercy. When a waitress spills hot coffee onto your hand instead of into your mug, you can show mercy. If a driver edges into your lane because he made a last-minute decision to exit, you are gifted with a mercy moment. The day a friend returns a borrowed, dry-clean-only sweater that is now shrunken and tiny, try mercy on for size.

I didn't say mercy was easy. I said it was gentle, courageous, and transforming. Share your new understanding of mercy when you are placed as judge or teacher or parent of another. Your mercy will generate the gift of peace for yourself and others.

Shedding Light

- When have you shown great mercy? When have you not shown compassion for another and regretted it later?
- Train your heart and mind on God's love so that mercy becomes your nature.
- If you enjoy or desire having power over someone else at work or at home, step back and give that situation to God in prayer. Chances are you'll need a pride adjustment.

Prayer

My fuse seems to be so short lately. God, grant me a heart that expresses real compassion. I know the truest, deepest, most transforming compassion because of your grace. Help me to pass it on…especially when my pride wants me to correct, limit, or judge another.

Afterglow

I'll extend grace and mercy to everyone I meet today.

Called to Immediate Action

I have found that among its other benefits,
giving liberates the soul of the giver.

MAYA ANGELOU

———✂———

Vivid documentaries of famine and poverty can move us to tears and compel us to send money to a cause based in a country we've never even visited. These are good impulses. But where many of us struggle with compassion is in our own circles, our own towns, and our community centers. The close proximity of poverty and pain can make us uncomfortable, even as our hearts ache for the need we see in our immediate areas. Spreading love and our resources to the ends of the earth is a good use of our time and our priorities, but we cannot do that and neglect sharing God's love with those closest to us.

Being a physical representative of Christ's love for another is a powerful act. When we first reach out to another person and touch their shoulder and look them in the eyes and express compassion, we will understand the importance of this personal, intimate connection with God's children. What does it look like to be Christ's hands? We are his hands and his heart when we are serving meals, reading mail to an elderly neighbor, giving someone money without conditions, offering to cook meals for a friend who is ill, holding hands with a person in the hospital, or listening to the needs and the life story of a stranger.

This isn't an easy or comfortable step for a lot of us. So we can pray and we can start by noticing the hearts and aches of the people in our own home. Then those of our neighbors. Then we can expand our awareness to the people we cross paths with on our way to work or at the bus stop. Loving those close to home with the unconditional love of Christ can change the world.

Shedding Light

- When you ask to see the needs and hurts of others...
  you will. Prepare to be prayerful and to draw from God's
  compassion.

- Have you wept for the heartache of another? Don't hold
  back from empathy. It connects you to the brokenness of
  others and then back to your own brokenness. Ultimately,
  it leads you right back to God's heart.

- Consider ways to be the hands of Christ. Preaching the
  gospel is for some...living the gospel is for all of us.

Prayer

God, where are those needs? I'm ready to see them and to respond to them. Even the people closest to me are good at hiding their pain and ignoring their need. Show me how to be vulnerable so that they are invited to do the same in my presence and in yours.

Afterglow

I won't turn away from those who are hurting, but I will reach out and make a connection.

One Car Over

We can choose to obey the still small stirring within, the little whisper that says, "Go. Ask. Reach out. Be an answer to someone's plea. You have a part to play. Have faith." We can decide to risk that He is indeed there, watching, caring, cherishing us as we love and accept love.

JOAN WESTER ANDERSON

———— ✦ ————

If you spend a few moments wondering who in your life might need prayer and are at a loss for someone to lift up, I think either the people in your life are experiencing amazingly good fortune or you are limiting your sense of neighbor too greatly. Could it very well be the latter? In our transitory society, our definition of neighbor should also be transitory. We can include those people we stand by at the post office or walk by on the way to our metro stop. We should include those who provide our mail, pick up our recycling, or deliver our favorite croissants to the corner coffee shop.

For me, it's good to ease into a spiritual philosophy shift slowly. I've started by considering the person or people one car over. It could contain anyone. A two-year-old having a meltdown in the backseat. A college student thumping their fingers on the steering wheel to the beat of a song while contemplating his purpose in life. A mother having a meltdown in the driver's seat. A woman heartbroken over the loss of her father. A father heartsick because this car has been his family's home since he lost his job last month. One car over is someone who needs prayer. Not because their life is a mess or on the brink of disaster, but because we all need prayer. We all need people to look at us through the compassionate eyes of a true neighbor.

Think differently and feel differently about the people who cross your route, even if just for the duration of a stoplight.

Shedding Light

- Who have you avoided becoming "neighbors" with? Reach out in a small way next time you have the chance.

- Prepare your heart to be more compassionate during your day. Spend moments in prayer in the morning. Read Scripture. Ask God to present you with the people who need a neighbor's awareness and kindness.

Prayer

That person next to me…here at the busy intersection…they cut me off three blocks ago. I don't know what they need, but you do. Cover them, guide them, give them a sense of peace today that steadies their heart and gives them a glimpse of hope.

Afterglow

I'll consider myself connected, responsible, and tied to others through compassion.

Jesus Loves Me

We are called to love the world. And God loved the
world so much that He gave Jesus. Today He loves
the world so much that He gives you and me to be
His love, His compassion, and His presence, through
a life of prayer, of sacrifice, of surrender to God.

MOTHER TERESA

———— ⦡ ————

The song "Jesus Loves Me" is a sweet tune that children learn in Sunday school, and yet its simple and radical truth can fill any adult with deep emotion. Oh, what it is to be loved so completely and so gently. This personal intimacy with God is one shared between all of God's children and their Creator. For some of us it is easy and logical to jump wholly and completely into the arms of the Divine. For others of us, it takes a longer time to be able to say "Jesus loves me" and to believe it on a soul level. But no matter when the truth of God's love does sink in, that great love envelops the heart and manifests in significant ways. Forgiveness in human relationships has new meaning. Connections to others are strengthened. The load of burdens is lessened. A sense of individual purpose replaces a random pursuit of success.

I take for granted the power of knowing that Jesus loves me, even though I rest in the comfort of that knowledge daily and cannot imagine life without that understanding. I know I am taking it for granted when I don't share it. The result of believing "Jesus loves me" should be visible fruits of service, generosity, grace, and mercy. When our hearts feel the compassion of Christ over and over, we know to go to God's reserve of patience and insight to keep on caring.

Knowing that Jesus loves me is my impetus to seek fellowship in this world even when it is awkward, hard, or uncomfortable. "Jesus loves me" is the powerful precursor to "Jesus loves you."

Shedding Light

- Has your head and heart knowledge of Jesus' love transformed the way you love others?

- What are some practical ways to say "Jesus loves you" to people you meet?

- Have you exchanged the pursuit of success for the pursuit of purpose?

Prayer

Lead me to transformed love, Lord. I come to you for patience and the strength to care for others. When I weigh the potential burden of helping another or supporting them in their time of need, remind me of the burdens you have taken from me. May I use my freedom to lead others to the same.

Afterglow

I will take the risk of deeper communion with a person in my life.

I Wish I Knew

When you get into a tight place and everything goes
against you, till it seems as though you could not
hang on a minute longer, never give up then, for that
is just the place and time that the tide will turn.

HARRIET BEECHER STOWE

I wish I knew what kept you up late staring at the dark while chasing shadows in your mind. You're dealing with stresses others aren't even aware of, and yet you keep a brave face until you are out of public viewing and in the solitude of nightfall. You're being brave so that the people you are caring for don't realize that their needs are overwhelming you. You're being brave because you haven't seen an alternative to being stoic and solid and always available to others.

I wish I knew which past hurt echoes through your soul today. You don't put it out there in conversation, even with close friends, because you think it would surprise and baffle people that the most poignant pain you ruminate over isn't the accident, illness, loss, or other "defining moment" that haunts you most. I'm not surprised. I understand that seemingly small hurts are the easiest ones to carry around in your heart's pocket and revisit every free moment.

I wish I knew what worry makes your heart skip a beat each time you step outside of your comfort zone. How the offhand comments of another leave your mouth dry and your palms sweaty. I imagine you have days that ticktock along like years because your energy is spent pretending you're fine and your hope is spent on survival instead of healing.

I wish you knew how much I pray to the One who does know every bit about you and who holds you in a great, protective embrace. Maybe this would bring you comfort. Maybe this would encourage you to allow that embrace to save you along this journey.

Shedding Light

- Who in your life doesn't know that the love of God is a personal, transforming love?

- Consider the way you hide your own loneliness or pain… most people you meet have those same hurts. Extend grace to those you encounter today.

- You can't always know what someone is going through, but God does. Trust his leading.

Prayer

Lord, I pray for those who have pain so deep that they barely make it through the day. Remove their loneliness and help them to seek out your heart and unconditional love. Give me a heart that is in line with your own so that I can offer up the right words and right actions people need.

Afterglow

When someone lashes out or pulls back, I will not take it personally, but will cover them in prayer.

Light a Candle
for Possibility

Birthing Pains

Each day you must say to yourself,
"Today I am going to begin."

JEAN PIERRE DE CAUSSADE

———————⌘———————

This is the year. My friends and I have felt that this could be the year we do more than merely contemplate and mull over our ideas. This could be the time in our lives when we put our ideas out into the world and see what can come of them.

The life of an idea begins at conception, but the power and influence of that idea begins when we send out the birth announcements. Unfortunately, many of us prolong the gestation period. Procrastinators, late bloomers, or those who believe they're not original, creative, or smart are the women with the longest gestations. Sorry to say this, but we're the elephants of the idea world. But I also have some good news for us. We, the plotters and the planners, are often the ones who give birth to the largest, strongest, most fascinating ideas. We just have to be willing to go through the labor pains.

Why is putting forth our ideas so painful, anyway? Why is it that we become afraid for our ideas to see the light of day? Personally, sometimes I'm afraid that the world will take one look at my idea and call it ugly…unworthy…puny. I believe that somewhere along the way we have forgotten that our ideas are part of God's creative purpose for our lives.

Follow through with the birthing of those ideas that grow within. You've been carrying them and protecting them. Now it's time to push them forth. Don't worry about what others will say about them. Just love them. Nurture them. See them as a wonderful, exciting extension of you, your heart, and the One who made you.

Shedding Light

- Are you gestating like an elephant? Isn't it time to birth that idea?

- Ideas aren't intended to be born full grown. They are supposed to be out in the world for a while before they are mobile or speak to others. You'll be able to nurture them as they grow.

- What holds you back from pushing your dreams forward?

Prayer

God, you give me dreams big and small. Guide me to follow your leading as I strive toward them. Connect me with others who will also nurture the dreams you want to see unfold in my life. May I strive to bring forth things of goodness and worth in your eyes.

Afterglow

This is the year...the week...the day, even...that I will give life to a new idea or to one that I've held close to my heart for far too long.

What to Pack for Time Travel

*Lives based on having are less free than
lives based on either doing or being.*

WILLIAM JAMES

It's midnight and I await 12:01 to mark the start of a new year.
Straddling two years makes me feel like a time traveler. I hear
fireworks. (I always wonder who sends those lights and sounds
skyward for the holiday.) And yet there have been many eves on
which I've been in the REM state of slumber when the actual
changeover from old to new has taken place. I never thought I
missed out on much, but I was wrong. When I stay awake and
ponder what it means to begin again, I discover a great sense
of optimism. Who are we if not beings who like beginnings?
We don't always enjoy the work involved with starting over, but
the appeal of a fresh start is strong for most of us.

Make the most of a new day. Apply a rush of optimism to
aspects of your life that are staid and stagnant. If you are standing on the dividing line between what is past and what can be,
how do you hope things will be different as you step fully into
the present and set your sights on the future? What or whom
should you let go of? I like to examine those things I should
pare away from my attitude (sarcasm, apathy) and my posses-
sions (clothes, unused workout equipment). Then it is fruitful
to prayerfully consider what I should be adding to my life in

the form of activities (volunteer opportunities), concerns (community health care), and dreams (travel, write).

Life is precious. Don't wait for the transition to a new year to consider what you can get rid of, what you are lacking, and what you are grateful for. Every morning you are traveling through time…it happens to be through your today. Only carry with you that which matters. And don't regret leaving a few things in the care of yesterday.

Shedding Light

- Think of one of your beginnings and how much it added to your life. What did it lead to?

- Do you straddle yesterday and today? Make the jump to today and see what you can do when your priorities and sensibilities are not divided.

- What do you think God wants you to leave behind? What are you supposed to take with you as you move forward?

Prayer

This or that? That or this? God, help me decide what to take with me as I press on toward possibility. Fill me with the light of optimism. I want to cherish my time, I want to savor my life, I want to live the gift of today.

Afterglow

I'll make a fresh start today and embrace the possibility of possibility!

Not a Spirit of Timidity

Don't trust to hold God's hand; let Him hold yours.
Let Him do the holding, and you the trusting.

HAMMER WILLIAM WEBB-PEPLOE

What's with the humidity in this room? Maybe I can leave early, I think as beads of sweat emerge at my hairline and along the curve of my neck. *Why did I come? Isn't it hot in here?* My throat is dry. This isn't an airborne disease entering my system. This is the power of timidity taking over my sense of courage and value at a social function. I don't have breakdowns, mind you. I tend to hold my own at gatherings, but typically a sense of dread rather than anticipation covers me when joining a group of most any kind. The symptoms kick in: awkwardness, fatigue, and a sense of fight or flight that takes over my thought process and apparently my sweat glands.

Can you relate? For many women, timidity can be the shadow that covers their moments to shine and to grow. It pulls them back when they are ready to express their opinions, heart, ideas, or their faith. Timidity can feel like the humidity of the Gulf Coast, but it isn't something we acclimate to or move away from. It follows us wherever we go until we take on God's strength and become empowered to be the unique, valued individual we have been created to be. God doesn't want us to hold back; he wants us to express who we are and who he is with passion and confidence. I have no problem voicing my opinion, yet I give over my confidence to that warped voice inside that says I'm not the person I should be. Send that warped voice out for ice and listen for the still, small voice of God. He'll set you straight and tell you *You are loved. You are mine. You have my strength. It's time to shine.*

Shedding Light

- Which situations stir up your timidity? How have you handled those times in the past?

- What does your warped inner voice say sometimes? What is God saying above (or below) the din of that negative narrator?

- Know without a doubt that you are loved, you are God's child, and you live in his strength.

Prayer

I trust you with my days, God. I can barely see beyond the current hour, but you see through eternity. I give you every part of me. Do something—anything—with this spirit of timidity I've adopted. I'm ready to step into your purpose with divine confidence.

Afterglow

I will not be afraid of the times I am supposed to shine.

Who Needs Whom?

God does not die when we cease to believe in a personal deity, but we die on the day when our lives cease to be illuminated by the steady radiance, renewed daily, of a wonder, the source of which is beyond all reason.

Dag Hammarskjöld

~~~

As you make choices, care for your family, and plot plans for the future, whose guidance are you seeking daily? When trouble rains down and your heart is laden with sorrow, whom do you trust to see you through to better times? As fear creeps into your rare moments of silence, whom do you turn to for peace? We quickly respond with "God, of course," because we do have faith. We know that God loves us and cares for us. We *know* this. But do we *live* as though we believe it?

Our time on this earth is amazingly precious and uncertain. Let's face it, we step out onto the front porch and we don't know what will happen next in our day. We can guess. We can hope. But we don't know. Doesn't it make sense to seek the leading of our all-knowing Creator? When we are waiting for faith to run deep in our lives, it is not because God needs time to become more real, more omniscient, more powerful. God has been God for a long time. He isn't waiting for us to truly believe in him before he can finally get some work done in the world. When we wait to believe completely, we miss our chance to live in God's purpose. When we leave everything to whimsy, emotion, or our own strength, we miss out on God's leading and clarity.

The current of "unknowing" in our lives is not meant to sweep us to places of fear and failure. The unknowing is the miracle that leads us to the wonder and mystery of a God who cares for us. Don't just know of God and about God; live in God. Experience the excitement and possibility lying beneath life's uncertainties when you wholly trust the known God.

Shedding Light

- When you disconnect from God's leading, he remains the Almighty...but you lose the power of the Creator in your life. Stay in touch with him. Remain linked to his strength and intention.

- Whims are fun to pursue for a Saturday afternoon, but not for a lifetime. Don't let your emotions rule your life. God has so much planned for it.

- Embrace the "unknowing" as a chance to trust God with every decision and every hope.

Prayer

I want my faith to run deep and true. God, show me the possibility of living in your purpose, even as I face uncertainty.

Afterglow

I will live as one who knows wholly and completely and without a doubt that God loves me.

Light at the End
of the Tunnel Vision

*When one door closes, another opens, but we often
look so long and so regretfully upon the closed door
that we do not see the one which has opened for us.*

ALEXANDER GRAHAM BELL

Have you ever gone back and retouched a resolution, so that you appeared to be closer to your aspiration? That never satisfies (not that I've tried such a thing, of course). It is quite unfortunate when we stand and stare at the path not taken, the job not explored, the relationship never initiated. These "undone" things feel more like losses than missed opportunities. We carry these perceived losses around with us, giving them weight and a sense of reality. But they are not truths, and they certainly shouldn't dictate your future or your today.

God must be saddened when he shines his light on our lives and sees us frozen with fear, big eyed, and unable to move toward the illuminated path. We are startled by a new direction being presented! It takes us by surprise because our eyes have been fixed on the things never pursued. I've never loved the pithy remark "When God closes a door, he opens a window." Why would God open a window when he can take the roof off of our house of cards? I don't think God goes to a downsized dream that fits through a smaller portal. This is the point in life when we should watch for the big hopes of a wide-open faith.

Be ready to move forward. And be prepared to leave a few things behind. Release your hold on regret; it won't serve you or God in the new venture. Decline an attitude of defeat; it doesn't belong in victorious living. Let go of last year's longings; they won't fit the new you. Now follow the light that radiates toward your future.

Shedding Light

- Are you afraid of what lies ahead? Even as God shines a light on your future? Take one step toward the horizon.

- Watch God take the roof off of your situation…in a good way. He'll reveal the expanse of the stars and the wonder of wide-open faith.

- Can you remove those "undone" things from your list of regrets? Allow them to be catalysts to embrace what you will do under God's leading.

Prayer

God, you define me. I won't give power over to the paths not taken…they lead nowhere! I will give power over to your vision and the light you shine on the way up ahead.

Afterglow

Today I will not consider defeat an option. I will be excited about and aware of how God is unfolding my life's potential.

Permission for Possibility

Your life is something opaque, not transparent,
as long as you look at it in an ordinary human way.
But if you hold it up against the light of God's goodness,
it shines and turns transparent, radiant and bright.

ALBERT SCHWEITZER

One day my husband told me that if something ever happened to him, I should quit my job, sell the house, and move to Paris to live and write for a year or more. I said, "Oh, don't talk like that," and then I said, "Thank you." I liked his dream for me because it suits me. And it meant that he was thinking about my passions. Later, I set aside the without-my-husband part of that scenario and took time to ponder what I would do with possibility. Travel. Write. Purge my belongings. Evaluate my priorities. Then I considered what I can do with possibility today—each and every one of those things! Yet why don't I?

How are you at pursuing the things on your heart? What are the leadings that drift in and out of your thoughts and prayers and times of silence, even when brief? Is your list similar to mine or radically different? Maybe you are one of the bold and courageous women who has strived to embrace her potential for many years.

All I know is that we need to stop tying our dreams to the anchor of impossibility and start whisking them along with the wings of possibility. God is the Creator and Fulfiller of endless opportunities, dreams, and visions. We should believe in horizons that open up our lives in ways that surpass our imaginations and hopes. Such experiences are the work of God. His signature is all over brilliant dreams realized. And his hope is behind ordinary dreams brilliantly realized.

I want us to taste that life beyond the excuses. No, I want us to breathe it, embrace it, and ultimately dive headfirst (noses not even plugged) into that life beyond doubt. Not that you need it, but you do hereby have my permission to dream and perceive possibility as a requirement for really living.

Shedding Light

- When you are alone with your thoughts and dreams… what are they?

- Do you give each day the weight it deserves? It is an entire day's worth of dreaming, living, and being as a child of God. It is significant!

- Release your hopes from the anchors of negativity and impossibility.

Prayer

Sometimes my hopes feel limited. It is almost as though I've given up on bigger dreams. I want to be alive with excitement and motivation again, God. I renew my hope in your brilliance. I renew my strength in your divine design.

Afterglow

I will hold my life up to the light of God's goodness.

Light a
Candle for the
Journey

Moving On

*It takes some of us a lifetime to learn that Christ,
our Good Shepherd, knows exactly what He is
doing with us. He understands us perfectly.*

PHILLIP KELLER

When my third grade teacher announced to my Iowa grade
school class that I was moving to Oregon, she pulled down
a large United States map, blue and green like the sea. She first
pointed to Iowa, nestled comfortably in the middle, and then
to a location so far on the left that she had to stretch her arm to
reach it. It seemed about as far from my childhood spot in the
universe as Mars. It was a visual that reinforced what I already
felt emotionally. *I'm leaving the center of the world.* Who wants
to say goodbye to the life they have known and start over?

As an adult I have several friends who have had to make big
moves. A couple of them faced significant geographic jumps
(I resisted unveiling a vinyl map and pointing out just how far
they were going), and the other had to make big shifts in career
pursuits. They each faced the big task and trial of sifting through
belongings. From shredding old bills and filing photos to wrap-
ping vases in bubble wrap, they prepared to pare down life so
that they were flexible enough to embark on a journey.

These times of moving on are difficult physically and spiritually. We grow roots in community, in familiarity, and in

security. These are all good and vital to our survival. But times of uprooting and transition are also part of survival and of goodness. When you can embrace a change in time zone rather than linger in your comfort zone, you will discover God's provision. When you can press on during a change in direction, you will discover God's faithfulness. When you are able to make God the center of your world instead of yourself, you are making strides toward a plan and purpose…even when you have to stretch your life to reach it.

Shedding Light

- Are you having to stretch your life so far that it hurts spiritually, emotionally, and physically right now? Have you ever?

- Do you trust God as the Shepherd of your life yet?

- Can you view changes in direction, location, or life patterns as a faith adventure? Each kind of change is a chance to grow in faith and discover the depths to which you can depend on God.

Prayer

Lord, I'm giving you my days, my needs, my choices, and my trust. Faith can be a bit scary, but I'm in this for good. I will walk in your way, and I will reach out to embrace the adventure of a lifetime.

Afterglow

I will view change as an opportunity to live more intentionally and to trust God more faithfully.

Escape Routes

*It helps me if I remember that God is
in charge of my day—not I.*

CHARLES R. SWINDOLL

———— ✑ ————

Backup plans are nice, even practical and healthy. I consider myself extremely mature and wise when I think through the best and worst case scenarios of a situation and chart out another path to success. But what is going on when we jump from strategically mapping out a backup plan to cleverly plotting a back *out* plan?

You might be someone who follows through with every commitment and who never thinks in terms of finding the nearest exit when facing obligations or those events and activities that make you uncomfortable. But I bring this up because I personally like to have an escape route when I face a new situation or when I attend a gathering. There are times when I've scheduled another appointment after an event so that I have a forced cutoff point. I often rejoice when an activity is canceled, because when I get out of something I have a surge of excitement. It feels like a snow day in grade school. I anticipate the free time and the possibilities of how I'll fill it.

However, as rebellious and whimsical as they feel initially, our back out plans eventually black out our dates of availability for what God has planned for us. If we dictate exactly how our life should unfold, we are never open to what God's plan is for us. If we spend our energy searching for an "out," we will never be in God's will. When you step in to each new situation with an open mind and open heart, you will get the most out of it.

Let's put our energy toward mapping a way out of mind-sets and habits that keep our lives restricted and controlled. It will be the greatest escape of all.

Shedding Light

- Do you ever hope that events will be canceled or that you can bow out of a commitment?

- How have you tried to escape responsibilities or relationships? Why did you have that impulse?

- Entering a new situation is easier when you release control of the outcome. I know that's hard to do, but it works. Try it with something you are facing this week.

Prayer

God, you are the only backup and safety net I need. Help me to resist placing my expectations on people and moments of my life. I want to greet each possibility with an open mind and a trusting heart.

Afterglow

I will spend time praying for and mapping out a way to leave behind fear and move forward in faith.

Just Visiting

Teach us to number our days and recognize how
few they are; help us to spend them as we should.

PSALM 90:12 TLB

This past year I had the wonderful opportunity to spend
time in my birth state and town and also in the city where
I lived after college. One is small-town America and the other
is an urban expanse of blocks. During my nostalgic visits, the
simplest things triggered a deep sense of joy. A field of corn set
against a darkened summer storm sky. A girls' softball game and
the aroma of hot dogs from the snack shack. The brick building
where I had my first career position. The boarded-up windows
of a deli and pie shop that used to be my regular breakfast stop.
The pine plank–floored bedroom in my first childhood home.
Each piece of my past was enjoyable real estate to walk through,
but it also felt good to just be visiting. Not because I couldn't
see myself in these places again, but because we should never
take up residence in days gone by.

You might not walk along the town square of your youth,
but maybe you frequently return to a past incident, a time of
suffering or affliction, or even a happy time that you've been
trying unsuccessfully to recapture. There is much to learn from
the earlier legs of our journeys. Why do we have the humor
we do? Why do we say our *R*s or *O*s with a bit of an accent?

It's good to notice the things we have adopted permanently into our personality or our sense of priority, but we are never meant to live in our past.

God lives with you in the present. This morning is the one in which he greets you with leading and love. This afternoon God will plant a seed of hope in your situation of concern. This evening is when he eases your concerns and reminds you in the quiet of your many blessings. Today God is shaping you. Don't be tempted to live anywhere else.

Shedding Light

- Where do you reside during your day or sleepless nights? Are you lost in a past circumstances, or are you living out today as God leads?

- Think on those things that you are grateful to have brought along from your past…good habits, sensibilities, faith, etc.

Prayer

God, usher me into the present when I linger over the past too often or for too long. When I revisit my hurts, remind me of my healing. When I start to wish for times gone by to resurface… remind me that today is where you and I connect and where you are guiding my steps.

Afterglow

I will take up residence in my life as it is now so that I can celebrate what happens today and have hope in tomorrow.

What's Left Is the Living

*If you wish to possess finally all that is
yours, give yourself entirely to God.*

HADEWIJCH OF BRABANT

Imaginary Counselor: How are you doing since we last met?

You: I've been reaching out to others more and more. And I've
been going to God for gratitude.

IC: What are you giving back to God?

You: Like an offering?

IC: When you give to God, you open up your life to God's
abundance. What are you lifting up to God that matters
to you?

You: I might be a bit more grateful, but life is far from perfect.
How can I give to God when I've still got all of this…

IC: What? What holds you back?

You: I've got a lot of anger. I'm not proud of it. What could I
possibly give to God when my heart is hardened?

IC: You answered your question. Give God that anger.

You: That's brokenness and bitterness. That's not a gift.

IC: Oh, but it is. When something consumes you, it steals your heart away from God. When you give that anger to God, the true offering is what remains.

You: That can't be much. If I gave up that heartbreak and rage, I'd be empty. What good is that?

IC: Would you be empty or free?

You: Well, free I guess. But there's the void from the anger…

IC: What remains?

You: Just me.

IC: Exactly. This is the offering God has been waiting for.

Shedding Light

- Give your anger, regret, and other life barriers to God.

- How long have you put off giving all of yourself to God?

- God knows what you are clinging to for false security. Accept the peace of being known and give the rest of your days to God's leading.

Prayer

This is it…my worst and my best. I give you my excuses, fear, and any anger that has kept me from love and gratitude. I give you this day along with my future hope.

Afterglow

Even when I don't feel like I have much to give, I'll give everything I am to God.

Rebirth

*When I look at the galaxies on a clear night—when
I look at the incredible brilliance of creation, and
think that this is what God is like, then instead
of feeling intimidated and diminished by it, I
am enlarged…I rejoice that I am a part of it.*

MADELEINE L'ENGLE

Nobody wants to hear about or think about death. Our culture often deals with death through the method of denial. And the more we leave a topic to grow in a corner like the shadow monsters of our childhood, the less we're able to cope with it in a healthy way. Are you waiting for something uplifting? I have it to offer, I really do. A friend and I were talking about the idea of death being the beginning of new life…a rebirth. This friend had lost someone quickly. There wasn't time to ponder and reflect; she had to just "be" with this person whom she loved and help him die. It was a time of sadness but not of fear because she honored her friend's life and death by providing tenderness, stories, laughter, and her presence during his last days. She helped him let go of the world and embrace new life.

We shouldn't let anything take away the beauty of this rebirth. Not fear, not ignorance, not shame. The denial of our inevitable physical demise prevents us from seeing death as a significant, meaningful part of life. When you look to the sky and contemplate God and the universe…you are a part of it all. The wonder. The miracle. Do you realize that death is our last offering to God? It's the point in our journey when we can say, "Take me into your presence, Lord." And this "me" is the part of us that loves others, delights in a sunset, praises God for life, and prays to God for guidance—this is the "me" who knows the hurt of brokenness and the joy of healing and who is ready to be whole and wholly in the presence of God. A new being, a new beginning.

Shedding Light

- Nurture your soul and your connection to God.
- Honor the importance of a second birth.
- Don't give death the power that life is meant to have. When you deny the fact of death, you give it the force of fear.

Prayer

God, even now I can give you all of myself daily by trusting you and staying in communion with you. I know that you mourn our deaths, our suffering, and our limited time on earth…but you also welcome us into your presence forever. Thank you for the comfort of knowing that our last offering is lovingly received.

Afterglow

I will savor living in God's presence today so that I might understand the peace that will cover me when I face a second birth.

Potluck Faith in Action

Delight yourself in the Lord and he will
give you the desires of your heart.

PSALM 37:4

———————— ❧ ————————

That vision I had about hosting a potluck…well, it materialized. And, of course, it had nothing to do with me and my planning. It was all God's doing. I'm sure he realized that if I was ever going to put that idea in motion, it would take many months and maybe even some counseling. As much as I wanted to open up my home and life to others, I also knew I'd have to give up control and the need for things to be perfect. What took place was so much better because it was out of my control. All I had to do was say yes to the opportunity God carved out for me.

And wouldn't ya know it, this all came about on Christmas Day.

Snow and ice made the driving conditions unsafe for my husband and me to travel to be with family, so on Christmas Eve we made our final decision to remain at home. Then we called a few friends who were also staying in town and invited them to Christmas dinner.

I was full of gratitude for our home, friends, and for God's profound presence in our lives during the past year. All day I was aware that on a small, manageable scale the potluck vision had materialized. It wasn't the big chaotic event I first envisioned (and been scared by). It was a time of fellowship that unfolded simply and graciously. I know it is just the beginning of how that dream will take shape in my life.

Over time, God forms the desires of our hearts and also orchestrates how they will appear. It might take us a moment to recognize a longing fulfilled, a hope met, a prayer answered, but these realized dreams are appearing all the time. In the light of God's goodness and hope, you will see them for what they are: a gathering of gifts for your faith journey.

Shedding Light

- How has God unfolded a hope that has been on your heart? Take time to reflect on these happenings. They are not by accident. They are purposed, significant gifts.

- Do you have desires of the heart? Sometimes we operate on autopilot for so long that we forget to dream and to nurture those hopes. Give yourself time to consider what God is placing on your heart.

Prayer

Give me a heart for the desires and plans you have for me, God. May I greet each day as another 24 hours in which I can delight in those desires.

Afterglow

I will hold on to the hopes and dreams God gives to me…and I will move forward toward them with gratitude.

About the Author

Hope Lyda has worked in publishing for 13 years and is the author of numerous fiction and nonfiction titles, including the popular One-Minute Prayers series (more than 650,000 copies sold), *One Minute with God,* and *Prayers of Comfort for Those Who Hurt.* When Hope isn't helping others in their writing endeavors as an editor, she can be found working on her latest writing project at a local coffee shop or jotting down ideas on 3 x 5 cards or any piece of scrap paper that's handy. She and her husband live in Oregon.

Hope Lyda
1574 Coburg Rd. #145
Eugene, OR 97401-4802

Email: hopelyda@yahoo.com
Website: www.hopelyda.com

Other inspirational books by
Hope Lyda

～

One-Minute Prayers™
One-Minute Prayers™ for Wives
One-Minute Prayers™ for Women
One-Minute Prayers™ from the Bible
One-Minute Prayers™ to Start Your Day
One-Minute Prayers™ to End Your Day
Prayers of Comfort for Those Who Hurt

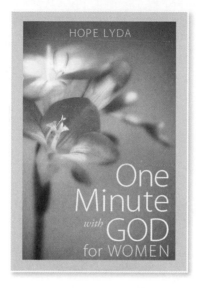

HOPE LYDA

One
Minute
with GOD
for WOMEN

Hope Lyda, author of the popular One-Minute Prayers series, shares inspiration and spiritual nourishment to help you experience more peace, contentment, and joy in your busy life. Along with Scriptures and prayers, this gathering of meditations provides the gifts of wonder and faith, deeper relationship with God, encouragement for tough stuff, and reminders of mercy and grace.

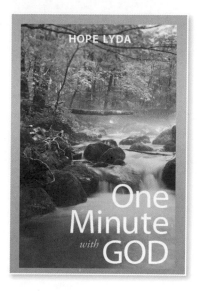

HOPE LYDA

One
Minute
with
GOD

Offering more moments of encouragement, reflection, and inspiration, Hope Lyda presents this delightful, heartwarming collection of devotions designed for your needs as a busy woman. Each engaging meditation offers refreshment and perspective for life's journey, connection with God, and the miracle of faith lived out daily.